90 DAYS OF
INTENTION
JOURNAL

The powerful research-backed method for achieving your big real estate investing goals in just ninety days.

BRANDON TURNER

BiggerPockets® PUBLISHING

90 Days of Intention Journal
Brandon Turner

Published by BiggerPockets Publishing LLC, Denver, CO
Copyright © 2018 by Brandon Turner.
All Rights Reserved.

This book belongs to

_____

WAIT!

Before starting, visit the link below to learn how to get the most out of this journal, as well as how to join an Intentional Mastermind Group!

www.BiggerPockets.com/start
Access Code: 90DAY

A LETTER FROM THE AUTHOR

Why do some individuals achieve incredible success? They live a life of great health, happiness, and financial independence—yet so many others struggle, fail, and give up on their dreams. Could it simply be that those who find success are intentional about finding it?

I'm Brandon Turner—real estate investor, bestselling author, and creator of this *90 Days of Intention Journal* from BiggerPockets—and I'm excited for the journey you are about to pursue.

As I was building my real estate business, I often struggled to keep up. Always reacting, always stumbling, always playing catch up. My finances suffered. My relationships were rocky. My physical health was far from ideal. I worked 100 hours a week, yet I was barely making progress on anything. I had too many goals, too little time, and no clear way to get the life I wanted.

But then something changed. I changed. I found intention for the kind of life I wanted to live. I wanted my real estate business to thrive. I wanted to look and feel healthy. I wanted to positively interact with friends, family, coworkers, and others. And over time, my intentions lead to actions which lead to real, lasting change.

What Everyone Gets Wrong About Change

Change, in any area of your life, is not made up of one or two big events. It's not a feeling. It's not a plan. Instead, lasting change is made up by small, repetitive actions taken every day. There's no fanfare. No parade. No trophies.

But for those who can identify their optimal routine, and create a system for accomplishing that routine, success is more generous than you can imagine! That's why the *90 Days of Intention Journal* was created: to help you identify those small actions, turn them into daily habits, and reach your highest potential.

Isn't it time you had the business, the relationships, the personal health, and the financial freedom you desire?

A Scientific Case for Success

Over the past several years, I've obsessed over one question: What separates successful achievers from those who give up, fail, or never get started?

Maybe you recognize that question from *The BiggerPockets Podcast*, because we've asked it to hundreds of guests. Over the past six years, we've seen certain patterns emerge from the inspiring stories of those who have found incredible success.

But, of course, causation doesn't always equal correlation. Do the daily habits, tactics, and routines of these highly successful people actually contribute to their success? Or is a by-product of their already successful nature? For that, we turned to cognitive science and psychology. We spent hundreds of hours researching books, published papers, and studies of human behavior to find what actually makes people successful in order to make this journal.

After years of study, the journal you hold in your hands is the result. It combines the best practices of top performers worldwide, as backed by the newest research into human potential. It's designed to keep track of your high-level 90-day goals, the weekly objectives you need to stay on track, your most important next step for each objective, end-of-day reflections on your progress, daily habit tracking, and much more.

In other words, this journal is going to help you accomplish your dreams in just a few minutes of daily, intentional writing.

Consider this your roadmap to the person you are about to become. It's time to live a life of intention, starting with the next 90 days. And BiggerPockets will be here for you the whole time.

Your friend,

Brandon Turner

INTRODUCTION PART I
HOW TO USE THIS JOURNAL

Chance didn't bring you to this journal.

Chance didn't encourage you to open it.

And chance isn't going transform the next 90 days of your life.

Intention will.

Whether you know it or not, the mere act of picking up this journal was a lesson in intentionality. You desire something better from your life, and you believe (as I do) that this journal will help you achieve it. So... you've already begun. Congratulations!

But before we get any further, it's time to walk you through how this journal is going to work. I know it's tempting to just jump in and begin, but let's take a few minutes to understand the why behind each section of this journal, along with how to fill it out to maximize your success.

How the Next 90 Days Look:
The *90 Days of Intention Journal* is designed to help you break your big goals down into the smallest parts, which increases your odds of accomplishing the big goal.

Wait... that's wrong, isn't it?

In reality, it's not about increasing your odds. This isn't chance. This isn't hope. This is intention. As Jim Rohn said, "If you really want to do something, you'll find a way. If you don't, you'll find an excuse." Therefore, this journal is designed to break your big goals down into the smallest parts, which increases your ability to make your dreams come true.

There... that sounds better!

We need to get rid of the idea that success is something that happens to us. Instead, let's consider success a direct result of our day-to-day actions. This journal is about taking big goals—which you will create in Part II—and working backwards to determine what those daily actions are. Then, you'll schedule them throughout your week and your day to move quickly and effectively toward the life you desire.

To do this, your journal contains two regularly updated sections:

1. The Weekly Battle Plan—The Weekly Battle Plan is a weekly strategy session designed to lift you out of the everyday muck, so you can survey your life like a general overseeing the battlefield. It's a place to work on your life, rather than in your life. This weekly section is imperative to an intentional life, as it will define the steps you take each day. I recommend completing this session at the start of each week (Sunday night or Monday morning) to launch you like a rocket into the next seven days. During this time, you'll write down your goals and a specific, tangible objective for the coming week, as well as the motivation for your objective and the roadblocks that could prevent you from reaching your goal.

The Weekly Battle Plan is also where you'll track and develop weekly habits. Want to read more? Track it. Want to analyze more deals? Track it. Finally, the Weekly Battle Plan includes an end-of-week review in which you can look back on the week and reflect. This section should take between 15-30 minutes to complete—but look at this time more as an "investment" than "time spent" because, due to the nature of intentional planning, you will save many otherwise wasted hours.

2. The Daily Action Plan—The Daily Action Plan is where you get in the trenches and fight the roadblocks. Each morning, you'll write down your three goals and weekly objectives to place yourself in the right mindset. You'll also identify your Most Important Next Step (M.I.N.S.), which is the large, actionable task you can do toward accomplishing your goal. (More on that in the introduction video at www. BiggerPockets.com/start.)

You'll also set a goal for your LAPS funnel (How many Leads are you going to seek today? How many deals will you Analyze? How many properties will your Pursue with an offer? How many deals will Succeed by closing?) Finally, you'll time-block your day, scheduling each moment so you run your day, rather than your day running you. The Daily Action Plan ends with an evening review, encouraging you to spend a few moments each night reflecting on the day to see what worked, what didn't, and what you can improve upon in the future.

The Weekly Battle Plan and The Daily Action Plan are your two greatest weapons in the battle for intention. Use them to transform your life over the next 90 days. By taking time each week and day to be intentional, you'll achieve amazing results: more free time, less stress, and new control over your life. That's the power of living intentionally.

INTRODUCTION PART II
THREE BIG GOALS

Research shows that having too many goals can be detrimental to accomplishing any of them. On the other hand, setting too few goals means not living up to your full potential.

That's why the *90 Days of Intention Journal* has space for three big goals. The first should be a real estate investing goal (as the journal is designed for real estate investors) and the other two can be whatever you desire (real estate-related or otherwise). Maybe it's weight loss, a work promotion, improving your relationships, or to run a marathon.

Each week, you'll write down your goals in the Weekly Battle Plan and once again in the Daily Action Plan. This may seem repetitive, but regularly reviewing your goals maximizes your focus to achieve them.

However, you need to set your goals before you can review them each day. Let's do that now!

90-Day Goal #1: _____

I will achieve this goal by (date): _____

I want to achieve this goal because: _____

_____

_____

_____

_____

_____

I will achieve this goal by doing these things: _____

_____

_____

_____

_____

90-Day Goal #2: _____

I will achieve this goal by (date): _____

I want to achieve this goal because: _____

_____

_____

_____

_____

_____

I will achieve this goal by doing these things: _____

_____

_____

_____

_____

_____

90-Day Goal #3: _____

I will achieve this goal by (date): _____

I want to achieve this goal because: _____

_____

_____

_____

_____

_____

I will achieve this goal by doing these things: _____

_____

_____

_____

_____

INTRODUCTION PART III
THE SEINFELD STRATEGY

Anyone who's tried their hand at stand-up comedy will tell you that most successful jokes do not come naturally. Instead, the best jokes emerge from hundreds or even thousands of jokes tested in front of real people. Some earn roaring laughter from every member of the audience, some elicit a polite chuckle, and the vast majority lead to nothing but crickets. Therefore, the key to a successful career in comedy is writing a lot of jokes, then fine tuning the best until you have a full set of killers.

Before finding mainstream fame as a television star, Jerry Seinfeld told jokes from the stage as a successful stand-up comedian. To compile his arsenal of jokes, he set a simple goal: Write every day and never miss a day. Seinfeld once told an up-and-coming comic to get a big wall calendar and a big red marker. For every day he did something toward his goal of becoming a comedian, he would cross out the day with a big red X. "After a few days you'll have a chain," Seinfeld told him. "Just keep at it and the chain will grow longer every day. You'll like seeing that chain, especially when you get a few weeks under your belt. Your only job next is to not break the chain."

This Seinfeld Strategy, of course, works for more than just jokes. Most big goals in life can be broken down to repetitive daily tasks. The more consistent you can be with those tasks, the closer you'll get to achieving the goal. For example, you can head to the gym one day a week and it will take years to achieve your fitness goals. But heading to the gym every single day will get you there a lot faster than if you never went at all. And the more consistently you complete a task, the more likely you are to continue that consistency. If you go to the gym 30 days in a row, chances are you won't miss day 31. Likewise, if you analyze one real estate deal each day for 60 days, how likely is it that you'll miss day 61?

This journal contains three Seinfeld Strategy boxes over 90 days with which you will define the "daily processes" that matter for your goals. Your daily processes can be related to your written goals or something peripheral. For example, you may want to track:

- A minimum amount of daily time spent on your real estate business
- Prospecting phone calls
- Days in the gym
- Deal analysis
- Driving for Dollars
- Education (books, podcasts, classes)
- Calories eaten

The point is, you can track anything that requires consistency. Simply place an "X" on each day you complete the task and leave blank each day you miss. Pretty soon, you'll build up a solid collection of Xs in a row, and the chance of skipping a day will be less likely. Be like Jerry and don't break the chain!

SEINFELD SQUARES

Numerous studies demonstrate the value of consistency in reaching your goals. Therefore, use the following chart to cross off each day you work on an action toward your goal. If you miss a day, leave the box empty. As you build up a "chain" of Xs, you'll be less likely to skip a day in the future.

GOAL ONE

Start here!

Keep going!

GOAL TWO

Start here!

Keep going!

GOAL THREE

Start here!

Keep going!

SAMPLE PAGES

The following pages contain a sample of what the Weekly Battle Plan and Daily Action Plan might look like. Feel free to use these as inspiration or ignore them and chart your own path.

This is your book. Start writing it!

WEEKLY BATTLE PLANNING

Week of _November 1st - November 6th_

GOAL REVIEW AND WEEKLY OBJECTIVES

Each week, review your big goals and subsequently break those goals down into objectives, determine the source of your motivation, identify potential roadblocks, and time-block those activities.

GOAL #1 Buy a single family rental property in Cincinnati by Dec 31st

This week, my objective is Send out 400 direct mail letters

I want this goal because I want financial freedom to spend more time with my kids

In pursuit of this objective, the largest roadblock might be I might not have the time to print all 400 letters

...and I'll overcome that roadblock by I'll hire my sister-in-law to print all the direct mail letters

I will work on this goal on Tuesday , at 3pm
(day)   (time)

GOAL #2 Lose 20 lbs by December 1st

This week, my objective is Lose 2 pounds

I want this goal because I want to live to see my great-grandkids, and look good for my wife!

In pursuit of this objective, the largest roadblock might be I might get too busy to work out or too busy to cook

...and I'll overcome that roadblock by putting three workouts on my calendar and planning my meals for the week

I will work on this goal on M, W, & F , at 6:30 am
(day)   (time)

GOAL #3 Find a real estate mentor

This week, my objective is Attend one local real estate meetup

I want this goal because I want financial freedom - but I know I'll need help. A mentor can help!

In pursuit of this objective, the largest roadblock might be I might be too nervous to attend a local event

...and I'll overcome that roadblock by Asking a friend to come with me

I will work on this goal on Friday , at 7pm
(day)   (time)

The #1 most important thing to move my real estate investing goals forward this week:	Send the direct mail letters. I HAVE to do this!

Now, go schedule this on your calendar.

SAMPLE WEEKLY RIGHT PAGE

BUILDING AND TRACKING DAILY HABITS

Use the foliong chart to identify three-to-six key habits or processes that, when carried out consistently, will result in positive changes and help you achieve your goals. In the first column, identify the habit; in the second, set a goal for the number of times you wish to accomplish this, and then track your progress throughout the week.

Habit/Process	Goal	SUNDAY	MONDAY	TUESDAY	WEDNESDAY	THURSDAY	FRIDAY	SATURDAY	Total
Analyze a deal	5	0	2	0	3	1	0	0	6!
Review my goals	7	x	x		x	x	x		5
Exercise 30 mins	3	x		x		x			3
Eat 2,000 cal	5	x	x		x	x	x	x	6!
Read 30 mins	4	x	x				x		3
Listen to BP podcast	2		x			x			2

END OF WEEK REVIEW

Looking at your wins and losses from your recent past can help you identify patterns, celebrate wins, determine course corrections, and ultimately lead you closer to your destination.

How did I get closer to my real estate investing goals this week?   **I sent out the direct mail letters!**

What lessons did I learn this week that will help me next week?   **I learned that I don't need to reinvent the wheel.**
I can just find out what works for other people, in similar markets, and do the same. It worked this week!

On a scale of 1–10, with 10 being the highest, I would rate last week's productivity at a... 1 2 3 4 5 6 ⑦ 8 9 10

	YES	NO
Did I take care of my body and mind the right way this week?	☒	☐
Did I take care of my relationships the right way this week?	☒	☐
Did I take enough breaks and make time for myself this week?	☐	☒
Did I get enough sleep this week?	☐	☒

Last week I studied...
"How to Invest in Real Estate"

Next week I'll study...
"...Managing Rental Properties"

Did I accomplish my #1 most important goal last week?	**YES!**	If yes, celebrate! If not, why?	**Whoop whoop!**

SAMPLE DAILY PAGE LEFT

DAILY ACTION PLAN

Date: 11 / 02 / 18   S M T Ⓦ Th F S

"Successful people do what unsuccessful people are not willing to do.
Don't wish it were easier; wish you were better."

—Jim Rohn

MORNING ROUTINE

Wake-up time 6 am   Water ☒ Exercise ☒ Daily Journal ☒ breakfast ☒ meditation ☒

This morning, I'm grateful for the strong friendships I have with John and Jim

GOALS AND M.I.N.S

Goals are important to review daily, reinforcing your objectives to your conscious and subconscious mind. But goals alone are not enough. It's also vital that you take time to identify your Most Important Next Step (M.I.N.S.) for each goal, so your goal transforms into an action. And remember, when it comes to M.I.N.S., be specific.

Real Estate Goal: Buy a single family rental house by Dec 31st

Weekly Objective: Send out 400 direct mail letters

M.I.N.S. Call my sister-in-law and ask her to print these and mail them by Friday

Second Goal: Lose 20 lbs

Weekly Objective: Lose 2 lbs

M.I.N.S. Lay out my running shoes the night before and put my running shoes on my feet at 6:30am

Third Goal: Find a real estate mentor

Weekly Objective: Attend a local real estate event

M.I.N.S. Go to BiggerPockets.com/events and register for the local meetup – then call John

I can consider today a "win" if I Get the direct mail campaign out of my hands!

Now, go place this on your time-blocking calendar for today.

REAL ESTATE L.A.P.S. FUNNEL

Every real estate deal begins in a funnel, beginning with leads, moving down toward analysis, pursuing some, and finding success with a few.

High-achieving real estate investors identify the funnel, set goals, and work their funnel to achieve the number of properties they desire.

Use this space to set a daily goal for defining how you'll get leads, how many properties you'll analyze, how many properties you'll pursue (offer), and how many you'll purchase today.

GOAL		REALITY
400	LEADS	450!
5	ANALYZE	6!
0 offers this week	PURSUE	0
0 this week	$	0

SAMPLE DAILY PAGE RIGHT

TODAY'S TIME-BLOCKING ACTIVITIES

High-achieving real estate investors know that what gets scheduled gets done. Take a few minutes to think about your goals, your M.I.N.S., and schedule your day. Don't forget to include several breaks.

5AM–6AM	wake up @ 6, jog 30 mins	2PM–3PM	WORK - break at 2:30
6AM–7AM	shower/hair/family breakfast, etc.	3PM–4PM	WORK
7AM–8AM	read, then leave at 7:30 for work	4PM–5PM	drive home
8AM–9AM	WORK	5PM–6PM	Family time
9AM–10AM	WORK - break at 9:30	6PM–7PM	Family time - Dinner
10AM–11AM	WORK	7PM–8PM	Family time
11AM–12PM	WORK - break at 11:15	8PM–9PM	Analyze one property with BP Calculators
12PM–1PM	Call sister-in-law about direct mail - Lunch	9PM–10PM	TV with wife
1PM–2PM	WORK	10PM–11PM	lights out

[X] Did I include enough breaks in the day?   [X] Did I schedule my #1 most important thing?

EVENING REVIEW

Today was awesome because   I did my morning workout and I got my sister-in-law started on the direct
mail campaign.

Today I struggled with   Although I planned on family time from 5-8pm, I ended up on a work call for
45 minutes of that time. I need to set better boundaries with work/home life.

On a scale of 1–10, with 10 being the highest, I would rate today's productivity at a...   1 2 3 4 5 6 7 (8) 9 10

Tomorrow I will...
- jog four miles in the AM
- call John about the RE meetup
- stretch for twenty minutes
- clean the closet
- get groceries after work
- send a "thank-you note" to Monica

Other Thoughts/Notes
$250,000
x.7
$175,000

$175,000
-$35,000
$140,000

WEEKLY BATTLE PLANS

WEEKLY BATTLE PLANNING

Week of _____

GOAL REVIEW AND WEEKLY OBJECTIVES

Each week, review your big goals and subsequently break those goals down into objectives, determine the source of your motivation, identify potential roadblocks, and time-block those activities.

GOAL #1 _____

This week, my objective is _____

I want this goal because _____

In pursuit of this objective, the largest roadblock might be _____

...and I'll overcome that roadblock by _____

I will work on this goal on _____ , at _____

(day) (time)

GOAL #2 _____

This week, my objective is _____

I want this goal because _____

In pursuit of this objective, the largest roadblock might be _____

...and I'll overcome that roadblock by _____

I will work on this goal on _____ , at _____

(day) (time)

GOAL #3 _____

This week, my objective is _____

I want this goal because _____

In pursuit of this objective, the largest roadblock might be _____

...and I'll overcome that roadblock by _____

I will work on this goal on _____ , at _____

(day) (time)

The #1 most important thing to move my real estate investing goals forward this week:

Now, go schedule this on your calendar.

BUILDING AND TRACKING DAILY HABITS

Use the folioing chart to identify three-to-six key habits or processes that, when carried out consistently, will result in positive changes and help you achieve your goals. In the first column, identify the habit; in the second, set a goal for the number of times you wish to accomplish this, and then track your progress throughout the week.

Habit/Process	Goal	SUNDAY	MONDAY	TUESDAY	WEDNESDAY	THURSDAY	FRIDAY	SATURDAY		Total

END OF WEEK REVIEW

Looking at your wins and losses from your recent past can help you identify patterns, celebrate wins, determine course corrections, and ultimately lead you closer to your destination.

How did I get closer to my real estate investing goals this week? _____

_____

What lessons did I learn this week that will help me next week? _____

_____

On a scale of 1–10, with 10 being the highest, I would rate last week's productivity at a... 1 2 3 4 5 6 7 8 9 10

	Yes	No
Did I take care of my body and mind the right way this week?	☐	☐
Did I take care of my relationships the right way this week?	☐	☐
Did I take enough breaks and make time for myself this week?	☐	☐
Did I get enough sleep this week?	☐	☐

Last week I studied...

Next week I'll study...

Did I accomplish my #1 most important goal last week?

If yes, celebrate! If not, why?

WEEKLY BATTLE PLANNING

Week of _____

GOAL REVIEW AND WEEKLY OBJECTIVES

Each week, review your big goals and subsequently break those goals down into objectives, determine the source of your motivation, identify potential roadblocks, and time-block those activities.

GOAL #1 _____

This week, my objective is _____

I want this goal because _____

In pursuit of this objective, the largest roadblock might be _____

...and I'll overcome that roadblock by _____

I will work on this goal on _____ , at _____
                               (day)   (time)

GOAL #2 _____

This week, my objective is _____

I want this goal because _____

In pursuit of this objective, the largest roadblock might be _____

...and I'll overcome that roadblock by _____

I will work on this goal on _____ , at _____
                               (day)   (time)

GOAL #3 _____

This week, my objective is _____

I want this goal because _____

In pursuit of this objective, the largest roadblock might be _____

...and I'll overcome that roadblock by _____

I will work on this goal on _____ , at _____
                               (day)   (time)

The #1 most important thing to move my real estate investing goals forward this week:

Now, go schedule this on your calendar.

BUILDING AND TRACKING DAILY HABITS

Use the folioing chart to identify three-to-six key habits or processes that, when carried out consistently, will result in positive changes and help you achieve your goals. In the first column, identify the habit; in the second, set a goal for the number of times you wish to accomplish this, and then track your progress throughout the week.

Habit/Process	Goal	SUNDAY	MONDAY	TUESDAY	WEDNESDAY	THURSDAY	FRIDAY	SATURDAY	Total

END OF WEEK REVIEW

Looking at your wins and losses from your recent past can help you identify patterns, celebrate wins, determine course corrections, and ultimately lead you closer to your destination.

How did I get closer to my real estate investing goals this week? _____

_____

What lessons did I learn this week that will help me next week? _____

_____

On a scale of 1–10, with 10 being the highest, I would rate last week's productivity at a... 1 2 3 4 5 6 7 8 9 10

	Yes	No
Last week I studied...		
Did I take care of my body and mind the right way this week?	☐	☐
Did I take care of my relationships the right way this week?	☐	☐
Next week I'll study...		
Did I take enough breaks and make time for myself this week?	☐	☐
Did I get enough sleep this week?	☐	☐

Did I accomplish my #1 most important goal last week?

If yes, celebrate! If not, why?

WEEKLY BATTLE PLANNING

Week of _____

GOAL REVIEW AND WEEKLY OBJECTIVES

Each week, review your big goals and subsequently break those goals down into objectives, determine the source of your motivation, identify potential roadblocks, and time-block those activities.

GOAL #1 _____

This week, my objective is _____

I want this goal because _____

In pursuit of this objective, the largest roadblock might be _____

...and I'll overcome that roadblock by _____

I will work on this goal on _____ , at _____
                              (day)   (time)

GOAL #2 _____

This week, my objective is _____

I want this goal because _____

In pursuit of this objective, the largest roadblock might be _____

...and I'll overcome that roadblock by _____

I will work on this goal on _____ , at _____
                              (day)   (time)

GOAL #3 _____

This week, my objective is _____

I want this goal because _____

In pursuit of this objective, the largest roadblock might be _____

...and I'll overcome that roadblock by _____

I will work on this goal on _____ , at _____
                              (day)   (time)

The #1 most important thing to move my real estate investing goals forward this week:

Now, go schedule this on your calendar.

BUILDING AND TRACKING DAILY HABITS

Use the folioing chart to identify three-to-six key habits or processes that, when carried out consistently, will result in positive changes and help you achieve your goals. In the first column, identify the habit; in the second, set a goal for the number of times you wish to accomplish this, and then track your progress throughout the week.

Habit/Process	Goal	SUNDAY	MONDAY	TUESDAY	WEDNESDAY	THURSDAY	FRIDAY	SATURDAY	Total

END OF WEEK REVIEW

Looking at your wins and losses from your recent past can help you identify patterns, celebrate wins, determine course corrections, and ultimately lead you closer to your destination.

How did I get closer to my real estate investing goals this week? _____

_____

What lessons did I learn this week that will help me next week? _____

_____

On a scale of 1–10, with 10 being the highest, I would rate last week's productivity at a... 1 2 3 4 5 6 7 8 9 10

	Yes	No
Last week I studied...		
Next week I'll study...		
Did I take care of my body and mind the right way this week?	☐	☐
Did I take care of my relationships the right way this week?	☐	☐
Did I take enough breaks and make time for myself this week?	☐	☐
Did I get enough sleep this week?	☐	☐

Last week I studied...

Next week I'll study...

Did I accomplish my #1 most important goal last week? | | If yes, celebrate! If not, why?

WEEKLY BATTLE PLANNING

Week of _____

GOAL REVIEW AND WEEKLY OBJECTIVES

Each week, review your big goals and subsequently break those goals down into objectives, determine the source of your motivation, identify potential roadblocks, and time-block those activities.

GOAL #1 _____

This week, my objective is _____

I want this goal because _____

In pursuit of this objective, the largest roadblock might be _____

...and I'll overcome that roadblock by _____

I will work on this goal on _____ , at _____
                                         (day)   (time)

GOAL #2 _____

This week, my objective is _____

I want this goal because _____

In pursuit of this objective, the largest roadblock might be _____

...and I'll overcome that roadblock by _____

I will work on this goal on _____ , at _____
                                           (day)   (time)

GOAL #3 _____

This week, my objective is _____

I want this goal because _____

In pursuit of this objective, the largest roadblock might be _____

...and I'll overcome that roadblock by _____

I will work on this goal on _____ , at _____
                                           (day)   (time)

The #1 most important thing to move my real estate investing goals forward this week:

Now, go schedule this on your calendar.

BUILDING AND TRACKING DAILY HABITS

Use the folloing chart to identify three-to-six key habits or processes that, when carried out consistently, will result in positive changes and help you achieve your goals. In the first column, identify the habit; in the second, set a goal for the number of times you wish to accomplish this, and then track your progress throughout the week.

Habit/Process	Goal	SUNDAY	MONDAY	TUESDAY	WEDNESDAY	THURSDAY	FRIDAY	SATURDAY	Total

END OF WEEK REVIEW

Looking at your wins and losses from your recent past can help you identify patterns, celebrate wins, determine course corrections, and ultimately lead you closer to your destination.

How did I get closer to my real estate investing goals this week? _____

_____

What lessons did I learn this week that will help me next week? _____

_____

On a scale of 1–10, with 10 being the highest, I would rate last week's productivity at a... 1 2 3 4 5 6 7 8 9 10

	Yes	No

Last week I studied...

Next week I'll study...

Did I take care of my body and mind the right way this week? ☐ ☐

Did I take care of my relationships the right way this week? ☐ ☐

Did I take enough breaks and make time for myself this week? ☐ ☐

Did I get enough sleep this week? ☐ ☐

Did I accomplish my #1 most important goal last week?

If yes, celebrate! If not, why?

WEEKLY BATTLE PLANNING

Week of _____

GOAL REVIEW AND WEEKLY OBJECTIVES

Each week, review your big goals and subsequently break those goals down into objectives, determine the source of your motivation, identify potential roadblocks, and time-block those activities.

GOAL #1 _____

This week, my objective is _____

I want this goal because _____

In pursuit of this objective, the largest roadblock might be _____

...and I'll overcome that roadblock by _____

I will work on this goal on _____ , at _____
                              (day)   (time)

GOAL #2 _____

This week, my objective is _____

I want this goal because _____

In pursuit of this objective, the largest roadblock might be _____

...and I'll overcome that roadblock by _____

I will work on this goal on _____ , at _____
                              (day)   (time)

GOAL #3 _____

This week, my objective is _____

I want this goal because _____

In pursuit of this objective, the largest roadblock might be _____

...and I'll overcome that roadblock by _____

I will work on this goal on _____ , at _____
                              (day)   (time)

The #1 most important thing to move my real estate investing goals forward this week:

Now, go schedule this on your calendar.

BUILDING AND TRACKING DAILY HABITS

Use the folioing chart to identify three-to-six key habits or processes that, when carried out consistently, will result in positive changes and help you achieve your goals. In the first column, identify the habit; in the second, set a goal for the number of times you wish to accomplish this, and then track your progress throughout the week.

Habit/Process	Goal	SUNDAY	MONDAY	TUESDAY	WEDNESDAY	THURSDAY	FRIDAY	SATURDAY	Total

END OF WEEK REVIEW

Looking at your wins and losses from your recent past can help you identify patterns, celebrate wins, determine course corrections, and ultimately lead you closer to your destination.

How did I get closer to my real estate investing goals this week? _____

_____

What lessons did I learn this week that will help me next week? _____

_____

On a scale of 1–10, with 10 being the highest, I would rate last week's productivity at a... 1 2 3 4 5 6 7 8 9 10

	Yes	No
Last week I studied...		
Next week I'll study...		

Did I take care of my body and mind the right way this week? ☐ ☐

Did I take care of my relationships the right way this week? ☐ ☐

Did I take enough breaks and make time for myself this week? ☐ ☐

Did I get enough sleep this week? ☐ ☐

| Did I accomplish my #1 most important goal last week? | | If yes, celebrate! If not, why? | |

WEEKLY BATTLE PLANNING

Week of _____

GOAL REVIEW AND WEEKLY OBJECTIVES

Each week, review your big goals and subsequently break those goals down into objectives, determine the source of your motivation, identify potential roadblocks, and time-block those activities.

GOAL #1 _____

This week, my objective is _____

I want this goal because _____

In pursuit of this objective, the largest roadblock might be _____

...and I'll overcome that roadblock by _____

I will work on this goal on _____ , at _____
                              (day)   (time)

GOAL #2 _____

This week, my objective is _____

I want this goal because _____

In pursuit of this objective, the largest roadblock might be _____

...and I'll overcome that roadblock by _____

I will work on this goal on _____ , at _____
                              (day)   (time)

GOAL #3 _____

This week, my objective is _____

I want this goal because _____

In pursuit of this objective, the largest roadblock might be _____

...and I'll overcome that roadblock by _____

I will work on this goal on _____ , at _____
                              (day)   (time)

The #1 most important thing to move my real estate investing goals forward this week:

Now, go schedule this on your calendar.

BUILDING AND TRACKING DAILY HABITS

Use the folioing chart to identify three-to-six key habits or processes that, when carried out consistently, will result in positive changes and help you achieve your goals. In the first column, identify the habit; in the second, set a goal for the number of times you wish to accomplish this, and then track your progress throughout the week.

Habit/Process	Goal	SUNDAY	MONDAY	TUESDAY	WEDNESDAY	THURSDAY	FRIDAY	SATURDAY	Total

END OF WEEK REVIEW

Looking at your wins and losses from your recent past can help you identify patterns, celebrate wins, determine course corrections, and ultimately lead you closer to your destination.

How did I get closer to my real estate investing goals this week? _____

_____

What lessons did I learn this week that will help me next week? _____

_____

On a scale of 1–10, with 10 being the highest, I would rate last week's productivity at a... 1 2 3 4 5 6 7 8 9 10

	Yes	No

Last week I studied...

Next week I'll study...

Did I take care of my body and mind the right way this week? ☐ ☐

Did I take care of my relationships the right way this week? ☐ ☐

Did I take enough breaks and make time for myself this week? ☐ ☐

Did I get enough sleep this week? ☐ ☐

Did I accomplish my #1 most important goal last week?

If yes, celebrate! If not, why?

WEEKLY BATTLE PLANNING

Week of _____

GOAL REVIEW AND WEEKLY OBJECTIVES

Each week, review your big goals and subsequently break those goals down into objectives, determine the source of your motivation, identify potential roadblocks, and time-block those activities.

GOAL #1 _____

This week, my objective is _____

I want this goal because _____

In pursuit of this objective, the largest roadblock might be _____

...and I'll overcome that roadblock by _____

I will work on this goal on _____ , at _____
                                 (day)   (time)

GOAL #2 _____

This week, my objective is _____

I want this goal because _____

In pursuit of this objective, the largest roadblock might be _____

...and I'll overcome that roadblock by _____

I will work on this goal on _____ , at _____
                                 (day)   (time)

GOAL #3 _____

This week, my objective is _____

I want this goal because _____

In pursuit of this objective, the largest roadblock might be _____

...and I'll overcome that roadblock by _____

I will work on this goal on _____ , at _____
                                 (day)   (time)

> **The #1 most important thing to move my real estate investing goals forward this week:**

Now, go schedule this on your calendar.

BUILDING AND TRACKING DAILY HABITS

Use the folioing chart to identify three-to-six key habits or processes that, when carried out consistently, will result in positive changes and help you achieve your goals. In the first column, identify the habit; in the second, set a goal for the number of times you wish to accomplish this, and then track your progress throughout the week.

Habit/Process	Goal	SUNDAY	MONDAY	TUESDAY	WEDNESDAY	THURSDAY	FRIDAY	SATURDAY	Total

END OF WEEK REVIEW

Looking at your wins and losses from your recent past can help you identify patterns, celebrate wins, determine course corrections, and ultimately lead you closer to your destination.

How did I get closer to my real estate investing goals this week? _____

_____

What lessons did I learn this week that will help me next week? _____

_____

On a scale of 1–10, with 10 being the highest, I would rate last week's productivity at a... 1 2 3 4 5 6 7 8 9 10

	Yes	No
Did I take care of my body and mind the right way this week?	☐	☐
Did I take care of my relationships the right way this week?	☐	☐
Did I take enough breaks and make time for myself this week?	☐	☐
Did I get enough sleep this week?	☐	☐

Last week I studied...

Next week I'll study...

Did I accomplish my #1 most important goal last week?

If yes, celebrate! If not, why?

WEEKLY BATTLE PLANNING

Week of _____

GOAL REVIEW AND WEEKLY OBJECTIVES

Each week, review your big goals and subsequently break those goals down into objectives, determine the source of your motivation, identify potential roadblocks, and time-block those activities.

GOAL #1 _____

This week, my objective is _____

I want this goal because _____

In pursuit of this objective, the largest roadblock might be _____

...and I'll overcome that roadblock by _____

I will work on this goal on _____ , at _____
                              (day)   (time)

GOAL #2 _____

This week, my objective is _____

I want this goal because _____

In pursuit of this objective, the largest roadblock might be _____

...and I'll overcome that roadblock by _____

I will work on this goal on _____ , at _____
                              (day)   (time)

GOAL #3 _____

This week, my objective is _____

I want this goal because _____

In pursuit of this objective, the largest roadblock might be _____

...and I'll overcome that roadblock by _____

I will work on this goal on _____ , at _____
                              (day)   (time)

The #1 most important thing to move my real estate investing goals forward this week:	

Now, go schedule this on your calendar.

BUILDING AND TRACKING DAILY HABITS

Use the folioing chart to identify three-to-six key habits or processes that, when carried out consistently, will result in positive changes and help you achieve your goals. In the first column, identify the habit; in the second, set a goal for the number of times you wish to accomplish this, and then track your progress throughout the week.

Habit/Process	Goal	SUNDAY	MONDAY	TUESDAY	WEDNESDAY	THURSDAY	FRIDAY	SATURDAY	Total

END OF WEEK REVIEW

Looking at your wins and losses from your recent past can help you identify patterns, celebrate wins, determine course corrections, and ultimately lead you closer to your destination.

How did I get closer to my real estate investing goals this week? _____

_____

What lessons did I learn this week that will help me next week? _____

_____

On a scale of 1–10, with 10 being the highest, I would rate last week's productivity at a... 1 2 3 4 5 6 7 8 9 10

	Yes	No
Last week I studied...		
Did I take care of my body and mind the right way this week?	☐	☐
Did I take care of my relationships the right way this week?	☐	☐
Next week I'll study...		
Did I take enough breaks and make time for myself this week?	☐	☐
Did I get enough sleep this week?	☐	☐

Did I accomplish my #1 most important goal last week?

If yes, celebrate! If not, why?

WEEKLY BATTLE PLANNING

Week of _____

GOAL REVIEW AND WEEKLY OBJECTIVES

Each week, review your big goals and subsequently break those goals down into objectives, determine the source of your motivation, identify potential roadblocks, and time-block those activities.

GOAL #1 _____

This week, my objective is _____

I want this goal because _____

In pursuit of this objective, the largest roadblock might be _____

...and I'll overcome that roadblock by _____

I will work on this goal on _____ , at _____
                                 (day)   (time)

GOAL #2 _____

This week, my objective is _____

I want this goal because _____

In pursuit of this objective, the largest roadblock might be _____

...and I'll overcome that roadblock by _____

I will work on this goal on _____ , at _____
                                 (day)   (time)

GOAL #3 _____

This week, my objective is _____

I want this goal because _____

In pursuit of this objective, the largest roadblock might be _____

...and I'll overcome that roadblock by _____

I will work on this goal on _____ , at _____
                                 (day)   (time)

The #1 most important thing to move my real estate investing goals forward this week:

Now, go schedule this on your calendar.

BUILDING AND TRACKING DAILY HABITS

Use the folioing chart to identify three-to-six key habits or processes that, when carried out consistently, will result in positive changes and help you achieve your goals. In the first column, identify the habit; in the second, set a goal for the number of times you wish to accomplish this, and then track your progress throughout the week.

Habit/Process	Goal	SUNDAY	MONDAY	TUESDAY	WEDNESDAY	THURSDAY	FRIDAY	SATURDAY		Total

END OF WEEK REVIEW

Looking at your wins and losses from your recent past can help you identify patterns, celebrate wins, determine course corrections, and ultimately lead you closer to your destination.

How did I get closer to my real estate investing goals this week? _____

_____

What lessons did I learn this week that will help me next week? _____

_____

On a scale of 1–10, with 10 being the highest, I would rate last week's productivity at a... 1 2 3 4 5 6 7 8 9 10

	Yes	No

Last week I studied...

Next week I'll study...

Did I take care of my body and mind the right way this week? ☐ ☐

Did I take care of my relationships the right way this week? ☐ ☐

Did I take enough breaks and make time for myself this week? ☐ ☐

Did I get enough sleep this week? ☐ ☐

Did I accomplish my #1 most important goal last week?   If yes, celebrate! If not, why?

WEEKLY BATTLE PLANNING

Week of _____

GOAL REVIEW AND WEEKLY OBJECTIVES

Each week, review your big goals and subsequently break those goals down into objectives, determine the source of your motivation, identify potential roadblocks, and time-block those activities.

GOAL #1 _____

This week, my objective is _____

I want this goal because _____

In pursuit of this objective, the largest roadblock might be _____

...and I'll overcome that roadblock by _____

I will work on this goal on _____ , at _____
                              (day)   (time)

GOAL #2 _____

This week, my objective is _____

I want this goal because _____

In pursuit of this objective, the largest roadblock might be _____

...and I'll overcome that roadblock by _____

I will work on this goal on _____ , at _____
                              (day)   (time)

GOAL #3 _____

This week, my objective is _____

I want this goal because _____

In pursuit of this objective, the largest roadblock might be _____

...and I'll overcome that roadblock by _____

I will work on this goal on _____ , at _____
                              (day)   (time)

The #1 most important thing to move my real estate investing goals forward this week:

Now, go schedule this on your calendar.

BUILDING AND TRACKING DAILY HABITS

Use the folloing chart to identify three-to-six key habits or processes that, when carried out consistently, will result in positive changes and help you achieve your goals. In the first column, identify the habit; in the second, set a goal for the number of times you wish to accomplish this, and then track your progress throughout the week.

Habit/Process	Goal	SUNDAY	MONDAY	TUESDAY	WEDNESDAY	THURSDAY	FRIDAY	SATURDAY	Total

END OF WEEK REVIEW

Looking at your wins and losses from your recent past can help you identify patterns, celebrate wins, determine course corrections, and ultimately lead you closer to your destination.

How did I get closer to my real estate investing goals this week? _____

_____

What lessons did I learn this week that will help me next week? _____

_____

On a scale of 1–10, with 10 being the highest, I would rate last week's productivity at a... 1 2 3 4 5 6 7 8 9 10

	Yes	No
Last week I studied...		
Did I take care of my body and mind the right way this week?	☐	☐
Did I take care of my relationships the right way this week?	☐	☐
Next week I'll study... Did I take enough breaks and make time for myself this week?	☐	☐
Did I get enough sleep this week?	☐	☐

Did I accomplish my #1 most important goal last week? _____ If yes, celebrate! If not, why? _____

WEEKLY BATTLE PLANNING

Week of _____

GOAL REVIEW AND WEEKLY OBJECTIVES

Each week, review your big goals and subsequently break those goals down into objectives, determine the source of your motivation, identify potential roadblocks, and time-block those activities.

GOAL #1 _____

This week, my objective is _____

I want this goal because _____

In pursuit of this objective, the largest roadblock might be _____

...and I'll overcome that roadblock by _____

I will work on this goal on _____ , at _____
                              (day)   (time)

GOAL #2 _____

This week, my objective is _____

I want this goal because _____

In pursuit of this objective, the largest roadblock might be _____

...and I'll overcome that roadblock by _____

I will work on this goal on _____ , at _____
                              (day)   (time)

GOAL #3 _____

This week, my objective is _____

I want this goal because _____

In pursuit of this objective, the largest roadblock might be _____

...and I'll overcome that roadblock by _____

I will work on this goal on _____ , at _____
                              (day)   (time)

The #1 most important thing to move my real estate investing goals forward this week:

*Now, go schedule this on your calendar.

BUILDING AND TRACKING DAILY HABITS

Use the folioing chart to identify three-to-six key habits or processes that, when carried out consistently, will result in positive changes and help you achieve your goals. In the first column, identify the habit; in the second, set a goal for the number of times you wish to accomplish this, and then track your progress throughout the week.

Habit/Process	Goal	SUNDAY	MONDAY	TUESDAY	WEDNESDAY	THURSDAY	FRIDAY	SATURDAY	Total

END OF WEEK REVIEW

Looking at your wins and losses from your recent past can help you identify patterns, celebrate wins, determine course corrections, and ultimately lead you closer to your destination.

How did I get closer to my real estate investing goals this week? _____

_____

What lessons did I learn this week that will help me next week? _____

_____

On a scale of 1–10, with 10 being the highest, I would rate last week's productivity at a... 1 2 3 4 5 6 7 8 9 10

	Yes	No
Last week I studied...		
Did I take care of my body and mind the right way this week?	☐	☐
Did I take care of my relationships the right way this week?	☐	☐
Next week I'll study...		
Did I take enough breaks and make time for myself this week?	☐	☐
Did I get enough sleep this week?	☐	☐

Did I accomplish my #1 most important goal last week?

If yes, celebrate! If not, why?

WEEKLY BATTLE PLANNING

Week of _____

GOAL REVIEW AND WEEKLY OBJECTIVES

Each week, review your big goals and subsequently break those goals down into objectives, determine the source of your motivation, identify potential roadblocks, and time-block those activities.

GOAL #1 _____

This week, my objective is _____

I want this goal because _____

In pursuit of this objective, the largest roadblock might be _____

...and I'll overcome that roadblock by _____

I will work on this goal on _____ , at _____
                              (day)   (time)

GOAL #2 _____

This week, my objective is _____

I want this goal because _____

In pursuit of this objective, the largest roadblock might be _____

...and I'll overcome that roadblock by _____

I will work on this goal on _____ , at _____
                              (day)   (time)

GOAL #3 _____

This week, my objective is _____

I want this goal because _____

In pursuit of this objective, the largest roadblock might be _____

...and I'll overcome that roadblock by _____

I will work on this goal on _____ , at _____
                              (day)   (time)

The #1 most important thing to move my real estate investing goals forward this week:

Now, go schedule this on your calendar.

BUILDING AND TRACKING DAILY HABITS

Use the foloing chart to identify three-to-six key habits or processes that, when carried out consistently, will result in positive changes and help you achieve your goals. In the first column, identify the habit; in the second, set a goal for the number of times you wish to accomplish this, and then track your progress throughout the week.

Habit/Process	Goal	SUNDAY	MONDAY	TUESDAY	WEDNESDAY	THURSDAY	FRIDAY	SATURDAY	Total

END OF WEEK REVIEW

Looking at your wins and losses from your recent past can help you identify patterns, celebrate wins, determine course corrections, and ultimately lead you closer to your destination.

How did I get closer to my real estate investing goals this week? _____

_____

What lessons did I learn this week that will help me next week? _____

_____

On a scale of 1–10, with 10 being the highest, I would rate last week's productivity at a... 1 2 3 4 5 6 7 8 9 10

	Yes	No
Last week I studied...		
Next week I'll study...		

Did I take care of my body and mind the right way this week? ☐ ☐

Did I take care of my relationships the right way this week? ☐ ☐

Did I take enough breaks and make time for myself this week? ☐ ☐

Did I get enough sleep this week? ☐ ☐

| Did I accomplish my #1 most important goal last week? | | If yes, celebrate! If not, why? | |

WEEKLY BATTLE PLANNING

Week of _____

GOAL REVIEW AND WEEKLY OBJECTIVES

Each week, review your big goals and subsequently break those goals down into objectives, determine the source of your motivation, identify potential roadblocks, and time-block those activities.

GOAL #1 _____

This week, my objective is _____

I want this goal because _____

In pursuit of this objective, the largest roadblock might be _____

...and I'll overcome that roadblock by _____

I will work on this goal on _____ , at _____
                              (day)   (time)

GOAL #2 _____

This week, my objective is _____

I want this goal because _____

In pursuit of this objective, the largest roadblock might be _____

...and I'll overcome that roadblock by _____

I will work on this goal on _____ , at _____
                              (day)   (time)

GOAL #3 _____

This week, my objective is _____

I want this goal because _____

In pursuit of this objective, the largest roadblock might be _____

...and I'll overcome that roadblock by _____

I will work on this goal on _____ , at _____
                              (day)   (time)

The #1 most important thing to move my real estate investing goals forward this week:

Now, go schedule this on your calendar.

BUILDING AND TRACKING DAILY HABITS

Use the folloing chart to identify three-to-six key habits or processes that, when carried out consistently, will result in positive changes and help you achieve your goals. In the first column, identify the habit; in the second, set a goal for the number of times you wish to accomplish this, and then track your progress throughout the week.

Habit/Process	Goal	SUNDAY	MONDAY	TUESDAY	WEDNESDAY	THURSDAY	FRIDAY	SATURDAY	Total

END OF WEEK REVIEW

Looking at your wins and losses from your recent past can help you identify patterns, celebrate wins, determine course corrections, and ultimately lead you closer to your destination.

How did I get closer to my real estate investing goals this week? _____

_____

What lessons did I learn this week that will help me next week? _____

_____

On a scale of 1–10, with 10 being the highest, I would rate last week's productivity at a... 1 2 3 4 5 6 7 8 9 10

	Yes	No
Last week I studied...		
Did I take care of my body and mind the right way this week?	☐	☐
Did I take care of my relationships the right way this week?	☐	☐
Next week I'll study...		
Did I take enough breaks and make time for myself this week?	☐	☐
Did I get enough sleep this week?	☐	☐

Did I accomplish my #1 most important goal last week?

If yes, celebrate! If not, why?

DAILY ACTION PLANS

Date: ____ / ____ / ____ # DAILY ACTION PLAN S M T W Th F S

MORNING ROUTINE

Wake-up time _____ Water ☐ Exercise ☐ Daily Journal ☐ _____ ☐

This morning, I'm grateful for _____

GOALS AND M.I.N.S.

Goals are important to review daily, reinforcing your objectives to your conscious and subconscious mind. But goals alone are not enough. It's also vital that you take time to identify your Most Important Next Step (M.I.N.S.) for each goal, so your goal transforms into an action. And remember, when it comes to M.I.N.S., be specific.

Real Estate Goal: _____

Weekly Objective: _____

M.I.N.S. _____

Second Goal: _____

Weekly Objective: _____

M.I.N.S. _____

Third Goal: _____

Weekly Objective: _____

M.I.N.S. _____

I can consider today a "win" if I _____

Now, go place this on your time-blocking calendar for today.

REAL ESTATE L.A.P.S. FUNNEL

Use this space to set a daily goal for defining how you'll get **leads**, how many properties you'll **analyze**, how many properties you'll **pursue** (offer), and how many you'll **purchase** today.

GOAL   REALITY

LEADS

ANALYZE

PURSUE

$

TODAY'S TIME-BLOCKING ACTIVITIES

High-achieving real estate investors know that what gets scheduled gets done.
Take a few minutes to think about your goals, your M.I.N.S., and schedule your day.
Don't forget to include several breaks.

5AM–6AM _____	2PM–3PM _____
6AM–7AM _____	3PM–4PM _____
7AM–8AM _____	4PM–5PM _____
8AM–9AM _____	5PM–6PM _____
9AM–10AM _____	6PM–7PM _____
10AM–11AM _____	7PM–8PM _____
11AM–12PM _____	8PM–9PM _____
12PM–1PM _____	9PM–10PM _____
1PM–2PM _____	10PM–11PM _____

☐ Did I include enough breaks in the day?

☐ Did I schedule my #1 most important thing?

EVENING REVIEW

Today was awesome because _____

_____

Today I struggled with _____

_____

On a scale of 1–10, with 10 being the highest, I would rate today's
productivity at a...   1   2   3   4   5   6   7   8   9   10

Tomorrow I will...   Other Thoughts/Notes

_____   _____

_____   _____

_____   _____

_____   _____

_____   _____

_____   _____

Date: ____ / ____ / ____   # DAILY ACTION PLAN   S M T W Th F S

"You learn more from failure than success. Don't let it stop you.
Failure builds character."

—Anonymous

MORNING ROUTINE

Wake-up time _____   Water ☐   Exercise ☐   Daily Journal ☐   _____ ☐

This morning, I'm grateful for _____

GOALS AND M.I.N.S.

Goals are important to review daily, reinforcing your objectives to your conscious and subconscious mind. But goals alone are not enough. It's also vital that you take time to identify your Most Important Next Step (M.I.N.S.) for each goal, so your goal transforms into an action. And remember, when it comes to M.I.N.S., be specific.

Real Estate Goal: _____

Weekly Objective: _____

M.I.N.S. _____

Second Goal: _____

Weekly Objective: _____

M.I.N.S. _____

Third Goal: _____

Weekly Objective: _____

M.I.N.S. _____

I can consider today a "win" if I _____

Now, go place this on your time-blocking calendar for today.

REAL ESTATE L.A.P.S. FUNNEL

Use this space to set a daily goal for defining how you'll get **leads**, how many properties you'll **analyze**, how many properties you'll **pursue** (offer), and how many you'll **purchase** today.

GOAL   REALITY

LEADS

ANALYZE

PURSUE

$

TODAY'S TIME-BLOCKING ACTIVITIES

High-achieving real estate investors know that what gets scheduled gets done.
Take a few minutes to think about your goals, your M.I.N.S., and schedule your day.
Don't forget to include several breaks.

5AM–6AM _____	2PM–3PM _____
6AM–7AM _____	3PM–4PM _____
7AM–8AM _____	4PM–5PM _____
8AM–9AM _____	5PM–6PM _____
9AM–10AM _____	6PM–7PM _____
10AM–11AM _____	7PM–8PM _____
11AM–12PM _____	8PM–9PM _____
12PM–1PM _____	9PM–10PM _____
1PM–2PM _____	10PM–11PM _____

☐ Did I include enough breaks in the day?

☐ Did I schedule my #1 most important thing?

EVENING REVIEW

Today was awesome because _____

_____

Today I struggled with _____

_____

On a scale of 1–10, with 10 being the highest, I would rate today's
productivity at a...   1 2 3 4 5 6 7 8 9 10

Tomorrow I will...   Other Thoughts/Notes

DAILY ACTION PLAN

Date: _____ / _____ / _____

S M T W Th F S

"The way to get started is to quit talking and begin doing."
—WALT DISNEY

MORNING ROUTINE

Wake-up time _____ Water ☐ Exercise ☐ Daily Journal ☐ _____ ☐

This morning, I'm grateful for _____

GOALS AND M.I.N.S.

Goals are important to review daily, reinforcing your objectives to your conscious and subconscious mind. But goals alone are not enough. It's also vital that you take time to identify your Most Important Next Step (M.I.N.S.) for each goal, so your goal transforms into an action. And remember, when it comes to M.I.N.S., be specific.

Real Estate Goal: _____

Weekly Objective: _____

M.I.N.S. _____

Second Goal: _____

Weekly Objective: _____

M.I.N.S. _____

Third Goal: _____

Weekly Objective: _____

M.I.N.S. _____

I can consider today a "win" if I _____

Now, go place this on your time-blocking calendar for today.

REAL ESTATE L.A.P.S. FUNNEL

Use this space to set a daily goal for defining how you'll get **leads**, how many properties you'll **analyze**, how many properties you'll **pursue** (offer), and how many you'll **purchase** today.

GOAL   REALITY

LEADS

ANALYZE

PURSUE

$

TODAY'S TIME-BLOCKING ACTIVITIES

High-achieving real estate investors know that what gets scheduled gets done.
Take a few minutes to think about your goals, your M.I.N.S., and schedule your day.
Don't forget to include several breaks.

5AM–6AM	_____	2PM–3PM	_____
6AM–7AM	_____	3PM–4PM	_____
7AM–8AM	_____	4PM–5PM	_____
8AM–9AM	_____	5PM–6PM	_____
9AM–10AM	_____	6PM–7PM	_____
10AM–11AM	_____	7PM–8PM	_____
11AM–12PM	_____	8PM–9PM	_____
12PM–1PM	_____	9PM–10PM	_____
1PM–2PM	_____	10PM–11PM	_____

☐ Did I include enough breaks in the day?

☐ Did I schedule my #1 most important thing?

EVENING REVIEW

Today was awesome because _____

_____

Today I struggled with _____

_____

On a scale of 1–10, with 10 being the highest, I would rate today's
productivity at a...   1   2   3   4   5   6   7   8   9   10

Tomorrow I will...   Other Thoughts/Notes

_____   _____

_____   _____

_____   _____

_____   _____

_____   _____

_____   _____

Date: ____ / ____ / ____   **DAILY ACTION PLAN**   S M T W Th F S

"Don't let yesterday take up too much of today."
—WILL ROGERS

MORNING ROUTINE

Wake-up time _____   Water ☐   Exercise ☐   Daily Journal ☐   _____ ☐

This morning, I'm grateful for _____

GOALS AND M.I.N.S.

Goals are important to review daily, reinforcing your objectives to your conscious and subconscious mind. But goals alone are not enough. It's also vital that you take time to identify your Most Important Next Step (M.I.N.S.) for each goal, so your goal transforms into an action. And remember, when it comes to M.I.N.S., be specific.

Real Estate Goal: _____

Weekly Objective: _____

M.I.N.S. _____

Second Goal: _____

Weekly Objective: _____

M.I.N.S. _____

Third Goal: _____

Weekly Objective: _____

M.I.N.S. _____

I can consider today a "win" if I _____

Now, go place this on your time-blocking calendar for today.

REAL ESTATE L.A.P.S. FUNNEL

Use this space to set a daily goal for defining how you'll get **leads**, how many properties you'll **analyze**, how many properties you'll **pursue** (offer), and how many you'll **purchase** today.

GOAL   REALITY

LEADS

ANALYZE

PURSUE

$

TODAY'S TIME-BLOCKING ACTIVITIES

High-achieving real estate investors know that what gets scheduled gets done.
Take a few minutes to think about your goals, your M.I.N.S., and schedule your day.
Don't forget to include several breaks.

5AM–6AM _____	2PM–3PM _____
6AM–7AM _____	3PM–4PM _____
7AM–8AM _____	4PM–5PM _____
8AM–9AM _____	5PM–6PM _____
9AM–10AM _____	6PM–7PM _____
10AM–11AM _____	7PM–8PM _____
11AM–12PM _____	8PM–9PM _____
12PM–1PM _____	9PM–10PM _____
1PM–2PM _____	10PM–11PM _____

☐ Did I include enough breaks in the day?

☐ Did I schedule my #1 most important thing?

EVENING REVIEW

Today was awesome because _____

_____

Today I struggled with _____

_____

On a scale of 1–10, with 10 being the highest, I would rate today's
productivity at a...   1   2   3   4   5   6   7   8   9   10

Tomorrow I will...   Other Thoughts/Notes

DAILY ACTION PLAN

Date: ____ /____ /____   S M T W Th F S

"A pessimist sees the difficulty in every opportunity;
an optimist sees the opportunity in every difficulty."
—Winston Churchill

MORNING ROUTINE

Wake-up time _____   Water ☐   Exercise ☐   Daily Journal ☐   _____ ☐

This morning, I'm grateful for _____

GOALS AND M.I.N.S.

Goals are important to review daily, reinforcing your objectives to your conscious and subconscious mind. But goals alone are not enough. It's also vital that you take time to identify your Most Important Next Step (M.I.N.S.) for each goal, so your goal transforms into an action. And remember, when it comes to M.I.N.S., be specific.

Real Estate Goal: _____

Weekly Objective: _____

M.I.N.S. _____

Second Goal: _____

Weekly Objective: _____

M.I.N.S. _____

Third Goal: _____

Weekly Objective: _____

M.I.N.S. _____

I can consider today a "win" if I _____

Now, go place this on your time-blocking calendar for today.

REAL ESTATE L.A.P.S. FUNNEL

Use this space to set a daily goal for defining how you'll get **leads**, how many properties you'll **analyze**, how many properties you'll **pursue** (offer), and how many you'll **purchase** today.

GOAL   REALITY

LEADS

ANALYZE

PURSUE

$

TODAY'S TIME-BLOCKING ACTIVITIES

High-achieving real estate investors know that what gets scheduled gets done.
Take a few minutes to think about your goals, your M.I.N.S., and schedule your day.
Don't forget to include several breaks.

5AM–6AM _____	2PM–3PM _____
6AM–7AM _____	3PM–4PM _____
7AM–8AM _____	4PM–5PM _____
8AM–9AM _____	5PM–6PM _____
9AM–10AM _____	6PM–7PM _____
10AM–11AM _____	7PM–8PM _____
11AM–12PM _____	8PM–9PM _____
12PM–1PM _____	9PM–10PM _____
1PM–2PM _____	10PM–11PM _____

☐ Did I include enough breaks in the day?

☐ Did I schedule my #1 most important thing?

EVENING REVIEW

Today was awesome because _____

_____

Today I struggled with _____

_____

On a scale of 1–10, with 10 being the highest, I would rate today's
productivity at a...   1 2 3 4 5 6 7 8 9 10

Tomorrow I will...   Other Thoughts/Notes

Date: ____ / ____ / ____   # DAILY ACTION PLAN   S M T W Th F S

MORNING ROUTINE

Wake-up time _____   Water ☐   Exercise ☐   Daily Journal ☐   _____ ☐

This morning, I'm grateful for _____

GOALS AND M.I.N.S.

Goals are important to review daily, reinforcing your objectives to your conscious and subconscious mind. But goals alone are not enough. It's also vital that you take time to identify your Most Important Next Step (M.I.N.S.) for each goal, so your goal transforms into an action. And remember, when it comes to M.I.N.S., be specific.

Real Estate Goal: _____

Weekly Objective: _____

M.I.N.S. _____

Second Goal: _____

Weekly Objective: _____

M.I.N.S. _____

Third Goal: _____

Weekly Objective: _____

M.I.N.S. _____

I can consider today a "win" if I _____

Now, go place this on your time-blocking calendar for today.

REAL ESTATE L.A.P.S. FUNNEL

Use this space to set a daily goal for defining how you'll get **leads**, how many properties you'll **analyze**, how many properties you'll **pursue** (offer), and how many you'll **purchase** today.

GOAL   REALITY

LEADS

ANALYZE

PURSUE

$

TODAY'S TIME-BLOCKING ACTIVITIES

High-achieving real estate investors know that what gets scheduled gets done.
Take a few minutes to think about your goals, your M.I.N.S., and schedule your day.
Don't forget to include several breaks.

5AM–6AM _____	2PM–3PM _____
6AM–7AM _____	3PM–4PM _____
7AM–8AM _____	4PM–5PM _____
8AM–9AM _____	5PM–6PM _____
9AM–10AM _____	6PM–7PM _____
10AM–11AM _____	7PM–8PM _____
11AM–12PM _____	8PM–9PM _____
12PM–1PM _____	9PM–10PM _____
1PM–2PM _____	10PM–11PM _____

☐ Did I include enough breaks in the day?

☐ Did I schedule my #1 most important thing?

EVENING REVIEW

Today was awesome because _____

_____

Today I struggled with _____

_____

On a scale of 1–10, with 10 being the highest, I would rate today's productivity at a... 1 2 3 4 5 6 7 8 9 10

Tomorrow I will...

Other Thoughts/Notes

Date: ____ / ____ / ____   # DAILY ACTION PLAN   S M T W Th F S

MORNING ROUTINE

Wake-up time _____   Water ☐   Exercise ☐   Daily Journal ☐   _____ ☐

This morning, I'm grateful for _____

GOALS AND M.I.N.S.

Goals are important to review daily, reinforcing your objectives to your conscious and subconscious mind. But goals alone are not enough. It's also vital that you take time to identify your Most Important Next Step (M.I.N.S.) for each goal, so your goal transforms into an action. And remember, when it comes to M.I.N.S., be specific.

Real Estate Goal: _____

Weekly Objective: _____

M.I.N.S. _____

Second Goal: _____

Weekly Objective: _____

M.I.N.S. _____

Third Goal: _____

Weekly Objective: _____

M.I.N.S. _____

I can consider today a "win" if I _____

Now, go place this on your time-blocking calendar for today.

REAL ESTATE L.A.P.S. FUNNEL

Use this space to set a daily goal for defining how you'll get **leads**, how many properties you'll **analyze**, how many properties you'll **pursue** (offer), and how many you'll **purchase** today.

GOAL   REALITY

LEADS

ANALYZE

PURSUE

$

TODAY'S TIME-BLOCKING ACTIVITIES

High-achieving real estate investors know that what gets scheduled gets done.
Take a few minutes to think about your goals, your M.I.N.S., and schedule your day.
Don't forget to include several breaks.

5AM–6AM _____   2PM–3PM _____

6AM–7AM _____   3PM–4PM _____

7AM–8AM _____   4PM–5PM _____

8AM–9AM _____   5PM–6PM _____

9AM–10AM _____   6PM–7PM _____

10AM–11AM _____   7PM–8PM _____

11AM–12PM _____   8PM–9PM _____

12PM–1PM _____   9PM–10PM _____

1PM–2PM _____   10PM–11PM _____

☐ Did I include enough breaks in the day?   ☐ Did I schedule my #1 most important thing?

EVENING REVIEW

Today was awesome because _____

_____

Today I struggled with _____

_____

On a scale of 1–10, with 10 being the highest, I would rate today's
productivity at a...   1 2 3 4 5 6 7 8 9 10

Tomorrow I will...   Other Thoughts/Notes

DAILY ACTION PLAN

Date: ____ / ____ / ____

S M T W Th F S

"Creativity is intelligence having fun."
—Albert Einstein

MORNING ROUTINE

Wake-up time _____ Water ☐ Exercise ☐ Daily Journal ☐ _____ ☐

This morning, I'm grateful for _____

GOALS AND M.I.N.S.

Goals are important to review daily, reinforcing your objectives to your conscious and subconscious mind. But goals alone are not enough. It's also vital that you take time to identify your Most Important Next Step (M.I.N.S.) for each goal, so your goal transforms into an action. And remember, when it comes to M.I.N.S., be specific.

Real Estate Goal: _____

Weekly Objective: _____

M.I.N.S. _____

Second Goal: _____

Weekly Objective: _____

M.I.N.S. _____

Third Goal: _____

Weekly Objective: _____

M.I.N.S. _____

I can consider today a "win" if I _____

Now, go place this on your time-blocking calendar for today.

REAL ESTATE L.A.P.S. FUNNEL

Use this space to set a daily goal for defining how you'll get **leads**, how many properties you'll **analyze**, how many properties you'll **pursue** (offer), and how many you'll **purchase** today.

GOAL

REALITY

LEADS

ANALYZE

PURSUE

$

TODAY'S TIME-BLOCKING ACTIVITIES

High-achieving real estate investors know that what gets scheduled gets done.
Take a few minutes to think about your goals, your M.I.N.S., and schedule your day.
Don't forget to include several breaks.

5AM–6AM _____	2PM–3PM _____
6AM–7AM _____	3PM–4PM _____
7AM–8AM _____	4PM–5PM _____
8AM–9AM _____	5PM–6PM _____
9AM–10AM _____	6PM–7PM _____
10AM–11AM _____	7PM–8PM _____
11AM–12PM _____	8PM–9PM _____
12PM–1PM _____	9PM–10PM _____
1PM–2PM _____	10PM–11PM _____

☐ Did I include enough breaks in the day?

☐ Did I schedule my #1 most important thing?

EVENING REVIEW

Today was awesome because _____

_____

Today I struggled with _____

_____

On a scale of 1–10, with 10 being the highest, I would rate today's
productivity at a...   1   2   3   4   5   6   7   8   9   10

Tomorrow I will...   Other Thoughts/Notes

Date: _____ / _____ / _____ # DAILY ACTION PLAN S M T W Th F S

"Do what you can with all you have, wherever you are."
—THEODORE ROOSEVELT

MORNING ROUTINE

Wake-up time _____ Water ☐ Exercise ☐ Daily Journal ☐ _____ ☐

This morning, I'm grateful for _____

GOALS AND M.I.N.S.

Goals are important to review daily, reinforcing your objectives to your conscious and subconscious mind. But goals alone are not enough. It's also vital that you take time to identify your Most Important Next Step (M.I.N.S.) for each goal, so your goal transforms into an action. And remember, when it comes to M.I.N.S., be specific.

Real Estate Goal: _____

Weekly Objective: _____

M.I.N.S. _____

Second Goal: _____

Weekly Objective: _____

M.I.N.S. _____

Third Goal: _____

Weekly Objective: _____

M.I.N.S. _____

I can consider today a "win" if I _____

Now, go place this on your time-blocking calendar for today.

REAL ESTATE L.A.P.S. FUNNEL

GOAL   REALITY

Use this space to set a daily goal for defining how you'll get **leads**, how many properties you'll **analyze**, how many properties you'll **pursue** (offer), and how many you'll **purchase** today.

LEADS

ANALYZE

PURSUE

$

TODAY'S TIME-BLOCKING ACTIVITIES

High-achieving real estate investors know that what gets scheduled gets done.
Take a few minutes to think about your goals, your M.I.N.S., and schedule your day.
Don't forget to include several breaks.

5AM–6AM _____   2PM–3PM _____

6AM–7AM _____   3PM–4PM _____

7AM–8AM _____   4PM–5PM _____

8AM–9AM _____   5PM–6PM _____

9AM–10AM _____   6PM–7PM _____

10AM–11AM _____   7PM–8PM _____

11AM–12PM _____   8PM–9PM _____

12PM–1PM _____   9PM–10PM _____

1PM–2PM _____   10PM–11PM _____

☐ Did I include enough breaks in the day?   ☐ Did I schedule my #1 most important thing?

EVENING REVIEW

Today was awesome because _____

_____

Today I struggled with _____

_____

On a scale of 1–10, with 10 being the highest, I would rate today's
productivity at a...   1 2 3 4 5 6 7 8 9 10

Tomorrow I will...   Other Thoughts/Notes

_____   _____

_____   _____

_____   _____

_____   _____

_____   _____

_____   _____

Date: ____ / ____ / ____   # DAILY ACTION PLAN   S M T W Th F S

"It's not whether you get knocked down, it's whether you get up."
—Vince Lombardi

MORNING ROUTINE

Wake-up time _____   Water ☐   Exercise ☐   Daily Journal ☐   _____ ☐

This morning, I'm grateful for _____

GOALS AND M.I.N.S.

Goals are important to review daily, reinforcing your objectives to your conscious and subconscious mind. But goals alone are not enough. It's also vital that you take time to identify your Most Important Next Step (M.I.N.S.) for each goal, so your goal transforms into an action. And remember, when it comes to M.I.N.S., be specific.

Real Estate Goal: _____

Weekly Objective: _____

M.I.N.S. _____

Second Goal: _____

Weekly Objective: _____

M.I.N.S. _____

Third Goal: _____

Weekly Objective: _____

M.I.N.S. _____

I can consider today a "win" if I _____

Now, go place this on your time-blocking calendar for today.

REAL ESTATE L.A.P.S. FUNNEL

Use this space to set a daily goal for defining how you'll get **leads**, how many properties you'll **analyze**, how many properties you'll **pursue** (offer), and how many you'll **purchase** today.

GOAL   REALITY

LEADS

ANALYZE

PURSUE

$

TODAY'S TIME-BLOCKING ACTIVITIES

High-achieving real estate investors know that what gets scheduled gets done.
Take a few minutes to think about your goals, your M.I.N.S., and schedule your day.
Don't forget to include several breaks.

5AM–6AM _____	2PM–3PM _____
6AM–7AM _____	3PM–4PM _____
7AM–8AM _____	4PM–5PM _____
8AM–9AM _____	5PM–6PM _____
9AM–10AM _____	6PM–7PM _____
10AM–11AM _____	7PM–8PM _____
11AM–12PM _____	8PM–9PM _____
12PM–1PM _____	9PM–10PM _____
1PM–2PM _____	10PM–11PM _____

☐ Did I include enough breaks in the day?

☐ Did I schedule my #1 most important thing?

EVENING REVIEW

Today was awesome because _____

_____

Today I struggled with _____

_____

On a scale of 1–10, with 10 being the highest, I would rate today's
productivity at a...   1 2 3 4 5 6 7 8 9 10

Tomorrow I will...   Other Thoughts/Notes

DAILY ACTION PLAN

Date: ____ / ____ / ____

S M T W Th F S

*"People who are crazy enough to think they can change
the world are the ones who do."*

—ROB SILTANEN

MORNING ROUTINE

Wake-up time _____ Water ☐ Exercise ☐ Daily Journal ☐ _____ ☐

This morning, I'm grateful for _____

GOALS AND M.I.N.S.

*Goals are important to review daily, reinforcing your objectives to your conscious and
subconscious mind. But goals alone are not enough. It's also vital that you take time to
identify your Most Important Next Step (M.I.N.S.) for each goal, so your goal transforms
into an action. And remember, when it comes to M.I.N.S., be specific.*

Real Estate Goal: _____

Weekly Objective: _____

M.I.N.S. _____

Second Goal: _____

Weekly Objective: _____

M.I.N.S. _____

Third Goal: _____

Weekly Objective: _____

M.I.N.S. _____

I can consider today a "win" if I _____

Now, go place this on your time-blocking calendar for today.

REAL ESTATE L.A.P.S. FUNNEL

Use this space to set a daily goal for
defining how you'll get **leads**, how many
properties you'll **analyze**, how many
properties you'll **pursue** (offer), and how
many you'll **purchase** today.

GOAL   REALITY

LEADS

ANALYZE

PURSUE

$

TODAY'S TIME-BLOCKING ACTIVITIES

High-achieving real estate investors know that what gets scheduled gets done.
Take a few minutes to think about your goals, your M.I.N.S., and schedule your day.
Don't forget to include several breaks.

5AM–6AM _____	2PM–3PM _____
6AM–7AM _____	3PM–4PM _____
7AM–8AM _____	4PM–5PM _____
8AM–9AM _____	5PM–6PM _____
9AM–10AM _____	6PM–7PM _____
10AM–11AM _____	7PM–8PM _____
11AM–12PM _____	8PM–9PM _____
12PM–1PM _____	9PM–10PM _____
1PM–2PM _____	10PM–11PM _____

☐ Did I include enough breaks in the day?

☐ Did I schedule my #1 most important thing?

EVENING REVIEW

Today was awesome because _____

_____

Today I struggled with _____

_____

On a scale of 1–10, with 10 being the highest, I would rate today's
productivity at a...   1 2 3 4 5 6 7 8 9 10

Tomorrow I will...

Other Thoughts/Notes

Date: ____ / ____ / ____   # DAILY ACTION PLAN   S M T W Th F S

*"Failure will never overtake me if my determination
to succeed is strong enough."*
—Og Mandino

MORNING ROUTINE

Wake-up time _____   Water ☐   Exercise ☐   Daily Journal ☐   _____ ☐

This morning, I'm grateful for _____

GOALS AND M.I.N.S.

*Goals are important to review daily, reinforcing your objectives to your conscious and
subconscious mind. But goals alone are not enough. It's also vital that you take time to
identify your Most Important Next Step (M.I.N.S.) for each goal, so your goal transforms
into an action. And remember, when it comes to M.I.N.S., be specific.*

Real Estate Goal: _____

Weekly Objective: _____

M.I.N.S. _____

Second Goal: _____

Weekly Objective: _____

M.I.N.S. _____

Third Goal: _____

Weekly Objective: _____

M.I.N.S. _____

I can consider today a "win" if I _____

Now, go place this on your time-blocking calendar for today.

REAL ESTATE L.A.P.S. FUNNEL

Use this space to set a daily goal for
defining how you'll get **leads**, how many
properties you'll **analyze**, how many
properties you'll **pursue** (offer), and how
many you'll **purchase** today.

GOAL   REALITY

LEADS

ANALYZE

PURSUE

$

TODAY'S TIME-BLOCKING ACTIVITIES

High-achieving real estate investors know that what gets scheduled gets done.
Take a few minutes to think about your goals, your M.I.N.S., and schedule your day.
Don't forget to include several breaks.

5AM–6AM _____	2PM–3PM _____
6AM–7AM _____	3PM–4PM _____
7AM–8AM _____	4PM–5PM _____
8AM–9AM _____	5PM–6PM _____
9AM–10AM _____	6PM–7PM _____
10AM–11AM _____	7PM–8PM _____
11AM–12PM _____	8PM–9PM _____
12PM–1PM _____	9PM–10PM _____
1PM–2PM _____	10PM–11PM _____

☐ Did I include enough breaks in the day?

☐ Did I schedule my #1 most important thing?

EVENING REVIEW

Today was awesome because _____

_____

Today I struggled with _____

_____

On a scale of 1–10, with 10 being the highest, I would rate today's
productivity at a...   1 2 3 4 5 6 7 8 9 10

Tomorrow I will...   Other Thoughts/Notes

Date: ____ / ____ / ____   # DAILY ACTION PLAN   S M T W Th F S

"Security is mostly a superstition.
Life is either a daring adventure or nothing."
—HELEN KELLER

MORNING ROUTINE

Wake-up time _____   Water ☐ Exercise ☐ Daily Journal ☐ _____ ☐

This morning, I'm grateful for _____

GOALS AND M.I.N.S.

Goals are important to review daily, reinforcing your objectives to your conscious and subconscious mind. But goals alone are not enough. It's also vital that you take time to identify your Most Important Next Step (M.I.N.S.) for each goal, so your goal transforms into an action. And remember, when it comes to M.I.N.S., be specific.

Real Estate Goal: _____

Weekly Objective: _____

M.I.N.S. _____

Second Goal: _____

Weekly Objective: _____

M.I.N.S. _____

Third Goal: _____

Weekly Objective: _____

M.I.N.S. _____

I can consider today a "win" if I _____

Now, go place this on your time-blocking calendar for today.

REAL ESTATE L.A.P.S. FUNNEL

Use this space to set a daily goal for defining how you'll get **leads**, how many properties you'll **analyze**, how many properties you'll **pursue** (offer), and how many you'll **purchase** today.

GOAL   REALITY

LEADS
ANALYZE
PURSUE
$

TODAY'S TIME-BLOCKING ACTIVITIES

High-achieving real estate investors know that what gets scheduled gets done.
Take a few minutes to think about your goals, your M.I.N.S., and schedule your day.
Don't forget to include several breaks.

5AM–6AM	_____	2PM–3PM	_____
6AM–7AM	_____	3PM–4PM	_____
7AM–8AM	_____	4PM–5PM	_____
8AM–9AM	_____	5PM–6PM	_____
9AM–10AM	_____	6PM–7PM	_____
10AM–11AM	_____	7PM–8PM	_____
11AM–12PM	_____	8PM–9PM	_____
12PM–1PM	_____	9PM–10PM	_____
1PM–2PM	_____	10PM–11PM	_____

☐ Did I include enough breaks in the day?

☐ Did I schedule my #1 most important thing?

EVENING REVIEW

Today was awesome because _____

_____

Today I struggled with _____

_____

On a scale of 1–10, with 10 being the highest, I would rate today's
productivity at a...   1 2 3 4 5 6 7 8 9 10

Tomorrow I will...   Other Thoughts/Notes

DAILY ACTION PLAN

Date: _____ / _____ / _____

"Knowing is not enough; we must apply.
Wishing is not enough; we must do."
—Johann Wolfgang Von Goethe

MORNING ROUTINE

Wake-up time _____ Water ☐ Exercise ☐ Daily Journal ☐ _____ ☐

This morning, I'm grateful for _____

GOALS AND M.I.N.S.

Goals are important to review daily, reinforcing your objectives to your conscious and subconscious mind. But goals alone are not enough. It's also vital that you take time to identify your Most Important Next Step (M.I.N.S.) for each goal, so your goal transforms into an action. And remember, when it comes to M.I.N.S., be specific.

Real Estate Goal: _____

Weekly Objective: _____

M.I.N.S. _____

Second Goal: _____

Weekly Objective: _____

M.I.N.S. _____

Third Goal: _____

Weekly Objective: _____

M.I.N.S. _____

I can consider today a "win" if I _____

Now, go place this on your time-blocking calendar for today.

REAL ESTATE L.A.P.S. FUNNEL

Use this space to set a daily goal for defining how you'll get **leads**, how many properties you'll **analyze**, how many properties you'll **pursue** (offer), and how many you'll **purchase** today.

GOAL   REALITY

LEADS

ANALYZE

PURSUE

$

TODAY'S TIME-BLOCKING ACTIVITIES

High-achieving real estate investors know that what gets scheduled gets done.
Take a few minutes to think about your goals, your M.I.N.S., and schedule your day.
Don't forget to include several breaks.

5AM–6AM _____
6AM–7AM _____
7AM–8AM _____
8AM–9AM _____
9AM–10AM _____
10AM–11AM _____
11AM–12PM _____
12PM–1PM _____
1PM–2PM _____

2PM–3PM _____
3PM–4PM _____
4PM–5PM _____
5PM–6PM _____
6PM–7PM _____
7PM–8PM _____
8PM–9PM _____
9PM–10PM _____
10PM–11PM _____

☐ Did I include enough breaks in the day?

☐ Did I schedule my #1 most important thing?

EVENING REVIEW

Today was awesome because _____

_____

Today I struggled with _____

_____

On a scale of 1–10, with 10 being the highest, I would rate today's productivity at a...   1 2 3 4 5 6 7 8 9 10

Tomorrow I will...

_____
_____
_____
_____
_____
_____

Other Thoughts/Notes

_____
_____
_____
_____
_____

Date: ____ / ____ / ____   # DAILY ACTION PLAN

*"The only limit to our realization of tomorrow
will be our doubts of today."*
—FRANKLIN D. ROOSEVELT

MORNING ROUTINE

Wake-up time _____   Water ☐   Exercise ☐   Daily Journal ☐   _____ ☐

This morning, I'm grateful for _____

GOALS AND M.I.N.S.

*Goals are important to review daily, reinforcing your objectives to your conscious and
subconscious mind. But goals alone are not enough. It's also vital that you take time to
identify your Most Important Next Step (M.I.N.S.) for each goal, so your goal transforms
into an action. And remember, when it comes to M.I.N.S., be specific.*

Real Estate Goal: _____

Weekly Objective: _____

M.I.N.S. _____

Second Goal: _____

Weekly Objective: _____

M.I.N.S. _____

Third Goal: _____

Weekly Objective: _____

M.I.N.S. _____

I can consider today a "win" if I _____

Now, go place this on your time-blocking calendar for today.

REAL ESTATE L.A.P.S. FUNNEL

Use this space to set a daily goal for
defining how you'll get **leads**, how many
properties you'll **analyze**, how many
properties you'll **pursue** (offer), and how
many you'll **purchase** today.

GOAL   REALITY

LEADS

ANALYZE

PURSUE

$

TODAY'S TIME-BLOCKING ACTIVITIES

High-achieving real estate investors know that what gets scheduled gets done.
Take a few minutes to think about your goals, your M.I.N.S., and schedule your day.
Don't forget to include several breaks.

5AM–6AM _____   2PM–3PM _____

6AM–7AM _____   3PM–4PM _____

7AM–8AM _____   4PM–5PM _____

8AM–9AM _____   5PM–6PM _____

9AM–10AM _____   6PM–7PM _____

10AM–11AM _____   7PM–8PM _____

11AM–12PM _____   8PM–9PM _____

12PM–1PM _____   9PM–10PM _____

1PM–2PM _____   10PM–11PM _____

☐ Did I include enough breaks   ☐ Did I schedule my #1 most
   in the day?   important thing?

EVENING REVIEW

Today was awesome because _____

_____

Today I struggled with _____

_____

On a scale of 1–10, with 10 being the highest, I would rate today's
productivity at a...   1 2 3 4 5 6 7 8 9 10

Tomorrow I will...   Other Thoughts/Notes

DAILY ACTION PLAN

Date: ____ / ____ / ____

"What you lack in talent can be made up with desire,
hustle and giving 110 percent all the time."
—Don Zimmer

MORNING ROUTINE

Wake-up time _____   Water ☐   Exercise ☐   Daily Journal ☐   _____ ☐

This morning, I'm grateful for _____

GOALS AND M.I.N.S.

Goals are important to review daily, reinforcing your objectives to your conscious and subconscious mind. But goals alone are not enough. It's also vital that you take time to identify your Most Important Next Step (M.I.N.S.) for each goal, so your goal transforms into an action. And remember, when it comes to M.I.N.S., be specific.

Real Estate Goal: _____

Weekly Objective: _____

M.I.N.S. _____

Second Goal: _____

Weekly Objective: _____

M.I.N.S. _____

Third Goal: _____

Weekly Objective: _____

M.I.N.S. _____

I can consider today a "win" if I _____

Now, go place this on your time-blocking calendar for today.

REAL ESTATE L.A.P.S. FUNNEL

Use this space to set a daily goal for defining how you'll get **leads**, how many properties you'll **analyze**, how many properties you'll **pursue** (offer), and how many you'll **purchase** today.

GOAL   REALITY

LEADS

ANALYZE

PURSUE

$

TODAY'S TIME-BLOCKING ACTIVITIES

High-achieving real estate investors know that what gets scheduled gets done.
Take a few minutes to think about your goals, your M.I.N.S., and schedule your day.
Don't forget to include several breaks.

5AM–6AM _____	2PM–3PM _____
6AM–7AM _____	3PM–4PM _____
7AM–8AM _____	4PM–5PM _____
8AM–9AM _____	5PM–6PM _____
9AM–10AM _____	6PM–7PM _____
10AM–11AM _____	7PM–8PM _____
11AM–12PM _____	8PM–9PM _____
12PM–1PM _____	9PM–10PM _____
1PM–2PM _____	10PM–11PM _____

☐ Did I include enough breaks in the day?

☐ Did I schedule my #1 most important thing?

EVENING REVIEW

Today was awesome because _____

_____

Today I struggled with _____

_____

On a scale of 1–10, with 10 being the highest, I would rate today's productivity at a...   1 2 3 4 5 6 7 8 9 10

Tomorrow I will...   Other Thoughts/Notes

Date: ____ / ____ / ____   # DAILY ACTION PLAN

MORNING ROUTINE

Wake-up time _____   Water ☐   Exercise ☐   Daily Journal ☐   _____ ☐

This morning, I'm grateful for _____

GOALS AND M.I.N.S.

Goals are important to review daily, reinforcing your objectives to your conscious and subconscious mind. But goals alone are not enough. It's also vital that you take time to identify your Most Important Next Step (M.I.N.S.) for each goal, so your goal transforms into an action. And remember, when it comes to M.I.N.S., be specific.

Real Estate Goal: _____

Weekly Objective: _____

M.I.N.S. _____

Second Goal: _____

Weekly Objective: _____

M.I.N.S. _____

Third Goal: _____

Weekly Objective: _____

M.I.N.S. _____

I can consider today a "win" if I _____

Now, go place this on your time-blocking calendar for today.

REAL ESTATE L.A.P.S. FUNNEL

Use this space to set a daily goal for defining how you'll get **leads**, how many properties you'll **analyze**, how many properties you'll **pursue** (offer), and how many you'll **purchase** today.

GOAL   REALITY

LEADS

ANALYZE

PURSUE

$

TODAY'S TIME-BLOCKING ACTIVITIES

High-achieving real estate investors know that what gets scheduled gets done.
Take a few minutes to think about your goals, your M.I.N.S., and schedule your day.
Don't forget to include several breaks.

5AM–6AM _____   2PM–3PM _____

6AM–7AM _____   3PM–4PM _____

7AM–8AM _____   4PM–5PM _____

8AM–9AM _____   5PM–6PM _____

9AM–10AM _____   6PM–7PM _____

10AM–11AM _____   7PM–8PM _____

11AM–12PM _____   8PM–9PM _____

12PM–1PM _____   9PM–10PM _____

1PM–2PM _____   10PM–11PM _____

☐ Did I include enough breaks
in the day?

☐ Did I schedule my #1 most
important thing?

EVENING REVIEW

Today was awesome because _____

_____

Today I struggled with _____

_____

On a scale of 1–10, with 10 being the highest, I would rate today's
productivity at a...   1 2 3 4 5 6 7 8 9 10

Tomorrow I will...   Other Thoughts/Notes

_____   _____

_____   _____

_____   _____

_____   _____

_____   _____

_____   _____

Date: _____ / _____ / _____ # DAILY ACTION PLAN

*"The man who has confidence in himself
gains the confidence of others."*
—Hasidic Proverb

MORNING ROUTINE

Wake-up time _____ Water ☐ Exercise ☐ Daily Journal ☐ _____ ☐

This morning, I'm grateful for _____

GOALS AND M.I.N.S.

Goals are important to review daily, reinforcing your objectives to your conscious and subconscious mind. But goals alone are not enough. It's also vital that you take time to identify your Most Important Next Step (M.I.N.S.) for each goal, so your goal transforms into an action. And remember, when it comes to M.I.N.S., be specific.

Real Estate Goal: _____

Weekly Objective: _____

M.I.N.S. _____

Second Goal: _____

Weekly Objective: _____

M.I.N.S. _____

Third Goal: _____

Weekly Objective: _____

M.I.N.S. _____

I can consider today a "win" if I _____

Now, go place this on your time-blocking calendar for today.

REAL ESTATE L.A.P.S. FUNNEL

GOAL   REALITY

Use this space to set a daily goal for defining how you'll get **leads**, how many properties you'll **analyze**, how many properties you'll **pursue** (offer), and how many you'll **purchase** today.

LEADS

ANALYZE

PURSUE

$

TODAY'S TIME-BLOCKING ACTIVITIES

High-achieving real estate investors know that what gets scheduled gets done.
Take a few minutes to think about your goals, your M.I.N.S., and schedule your day.
Don't forget to include several breaks.

5AM–6AM _____	2PM–3PM _____
6AM–7AM _____	3PM–4PM _____
7AM–8AM _____	4PM–5PM _____
8AM–9AM _____	5PM–6PM _____
9AM–10AM _____	6PM–7PM _____
10AM–11AM _____	7PM–8PM _____
11AM–12PM _____	8PM–9PM _____
12PM–1PM _____	9PM–10PM _____
1PM–2PM _____	10PM–11PM _____

☐ Did I include enough breaks in the day?

☐ Did I schedule my #1 most important thing?

EVENING REVIEW

Today was awesome because _____

_____

Today I struggled with _____

_____

On a scale of 1–10, with 10 being the highest, I would rate today's
productivity at a...   1 2 3 4 5 6 7 8 9 10

Tomorrow I will...   Other Thoughts/Notes

Date: ___ / ___ / ___ # DAILY ACTION PLAN S M T W Th F S

"We generate fears while we sit. We overcome them by action."
—Dr. Henry Link

MORNING ROUTINE

Wake-up time _____ Water ☐ Exercise ☐ Daily Journal ☐ _____ ☐

This morning, I'm grateful for _____

GOALS AND M.I.N.S.

Goals are important to review daily, reinforcing your objectives to your conscious and subconscious mind. But goals alone are not enough. It's also vital that you take time to identify your Most Important Next Step (M.I.N.S.) for each goal, so your goal transforms into an action. And remember, when it comes to M.I.N.S., be specific.

Real Estate Goal: _____

Weekly Objective: _____

M.I.N.S. _____

Second Goal: _____

Weekly Objective: _____

M.I.N.S. _____

Third Goal: _____

Weekly Objective: _____

M.I.N.S. _____

I can consider today a "win" if I _____

Now, go place this on your time-blocking calendar for today.

REAL ESTATE L.A.P.S. FUNNEL

Use this space to set a daily goal for defining how you'll get **leads**, how many properties you'll **analyze**, how many properties you'll **pursue** (offer), and how many you'll **purchase** today.

GOAL   REALITY

LEADS

ANALYZE

PURSUE

$

TODAY'S TIME-BLOCKING ACTIVITIES

High-achieving real estate investors know that what gets scheduled gets done.
Take a few minutes to think about your goals, your M.I.N.S., and schedule your day.
Don't forget to include several breaks.

5AM–6AM _____	2PM–3PM _____
6AM–7AM _____	3PM–4PM _____
7AM–8AM _____	4PM–5PM _____
8AM–9AM _____	5PM–6PM _____
9AM–10AM _____	6PM–7PM _____
10AM–11AM _____	7PM–8PM _____
11AM–12PM _____	8PM–9PM _____
12PM–1PM _____	9PM–10PM _____
1PM–2PM _____	10PM–11PM _____

☐ Did I include enough breaks in the day?

☐ Did I schedule my #1 most important thing?

EVENING REVIEW

Today was awesome because _____

_____

Today I struggled with _____

_____

On a scale of 1–10, with 10 being the highest, I would rate today's
productivity at a...   1 2 3 4 5 6 7 8 9 10

Tomorrow I will...   Other Thoughts/Notes

DAILY ACTION PLAN

"Whether you think you can or think you can't, you're right."
—Henry Ford

MORNING ROUTINE

Wake-up time _____ Water ☐ Exercise ☐ Daily Journal ☐ _____ ☐

This morning, I'm grateful for _____

GOALS AND M.I.N.S.

Goals are important to review daily, reinforcing your objectives to your conscious and subconscious mind. But goals alone are not enough. It's also vital that you take time to identify your Most Important Next Step (M.I.N.S.) for each goal, so your goal transforms into an action. And remember, when it comes to M.I.N.S., be specific.

Real Estate Goal: _____

Weekly Objective: _____

M.I.N.S. _____

Second Goal: _____

Weekly Objective: _____

M.I.N.S. _____

Third Goal: _____

Weekly Objective: _____

M.I.N.S. _____

I can consider today a "win" if I _____

Now, go place this on your time-blocking calendar for today.

REAL ESTATE L.A.P.S. FUNNEL

Use this space to set a daily goal for defining how you'll get **leads**, how many properties you'll **analyze**, how many properties you'll **pursue** (offer), and how many you'll **purchase** today.

GOAL   REALITY

LEADS

ANALYZE

PURSUE

$

TODAY'S TIME-BLOCKING ACTIVITIES

High-achieving real estate investors know that what gets scheduled gets done.
Take a few minutes to think about your goals, your M.I.N.S., and schedule your day.
Don't forget to include several breaks.

5AM–6AM _____	2PM–3PM _____
6AM–7AM _____	3PM–4PM _____
7AM–8AM _____	4PM–5PM _____
8AM–9AM _____	5PM–6PM _____
9AM–10AM _____	6PM–7PM _____
10AM–11AM _____	7PM–8PM _____
11AM–12PM _____	8PM–9PM _____
12PM–1PM _____	9PM–10PM _____
1PM–2PM _____	10PM–11PM _____

☐ Did I include enough breaks in the day?

☐ Did I schedule my #1 most important thing?

EVENING REVIEW

Today was awesome because _____

_____

Today I struggled with _____

_____

On a scale of 1–10, with 10 being the highest, I would rate today's productivity at a...   1   2   3   4   5   6   7   8   9   10

Tomorrow I will...   Other Thoughts/Notes

_____   _____

_____   _____

_____   _____

_____   _____

_____   _____

_____   _____

DAILY ACTION PLAN

Date: ____ / ____ / ____

S M T W Th F S

MORNING ROUTINE

Wake-up time _____   Water ☐   Exercise ☐   Daily Journal ☐   _____ ☐

This morning, I'm grateful for _____

GOALS AND M.I.N.S.

*Goals are important to review daily, reinforcing your objectives to your conscious and
subconscious mind. But goals alone are not enough. It's also vital that you take time to
identify your Most Important Next Step (M.I.N.S.) for each goal, so your goal transforms
into an action. And remember, when it comes to M.I.N.S., be specific.*

Real Estate Goal: _____

Weekly Objective: _____

M.I.N.S. _____

Second Goal: _____

Weekly Objective: _____

M.I.N.S. _____

Third Goal: _____

Weekly Objective: _____

M.I.N.S. _____

I can consider today a "win" if I _____

Now, go place this on your time-blocking calendar for today.

REAL ESTATE L.A.P.S. FUNNEL

Use this space to set a daily goal for
defining how you'll get **leads**, how many
properties you'll **analyze**, how many
properties you'll **pursue** (offer), and how
many you'll **purchase** today.

GOAL   REALITY

LEADS

ANALYZE

PURSUE

$

TODAY'S TIME-BLOCKING ACTIVITIES

High-achieving real estate investors know that what gets scheduled gets done.
Take a few minutes to think about your goals, your M.I.N.S., and schedule your day.
Don't forget to include several breaks.

5AM–6AM _____   2PM–3PM _____

6AM–7AM _____   3PM–4PM _____

7AM–8AM _____   4PM–5PM _____

8AM–9AM _____   5PM–6PM _____

9AM–10AM _____   6PM–7PM _____

10AM–11AM _____   7PM–8PM _____

11AM–12PM _____   8PM–9PM _____

12PM–1PM _____   9PM–10PM _____

1PM–2PM _____   10PM–11PM _____

☐ Did I include enough breaks in the day?   ☐ Did I schedule my #1 most important thing?

EVENING REVIEW

Today was awesome because _____

_____

Today I struggled with _____

_____

On a scale of 1–10, with 10 being the highest, I would rate today's
productivity at a...   1 2 3 4 5 6 7 8 9 10

Tomorrow I will...   Other Thoughts/Notes

Date: ____ / ____ / ____   # DAILY ACTION PLAN   S M T W Th F S

"To see what is right and not do it is a lack of courage."
—CONFUCIUS

MORNING ROUTINE

Wake-up time _____   Water ☐   Exercise ☐   Daily Journal ☐   _____ ☐

This morning, I'm grateful for _____

GOALS AND M.I.N.S.

Goals are important to review daily, reinforcing your objectives to your conscious and subconscious mind. But goals alone are not enough. It's also vital that you take time to identify your Most Important Next Step (M.I.N.S.) for each goal, so your goal transforms into an action. And remember, when it comes to M.I.N.S., be specific.

Real Estate Goal: _____

Weekly Objective: _____

M.I.N.S. _____

Second Goal: _____

Weekly Objective: _____

M.I.N.S. _____

Third Goal: _____

Weekly Objective: _____

M.I.N.S. _____

I can consider today a "win" if I _____

Now, go place this on your time-blocking calendar for today.

REAL ESTATE L.A.P.S. FUNNEL

Use this space to set a daily goal for defining how you'll get **leads**, how many properties you'll **analyze**, how many properties you'll **pursue** (offer), and how many you'll **purchase** today.

GOAL   REALITY

LEADS

ANALYZE

PURSUE

$

TODAY'S TIME-BLOCKING ACTIVITIES

High-achieving real estate investors know that what gets scheduled gets done.
Take a few minutes to think about your goals, your M.I.N.S., and schedule your day.
Don't forget to include several breaks.

5AM–6AM _____	2PM–3PM _____
6AM–7AM _____	3PM–4PM _____
7AM–8AM _____	4PM–5PM _____
8AM–9AM _____	5PM–6PM _____
9AM–10AM _____	6PM–7PM _____
10AM–11AM _____	7PM–8PM _____
11AM–12PM _____	8PM–9PM _____
12PM–1PM _____	9PM–10PM _____
1PM–2PM _____	10PM–11PM _____

☐ Did I include enough breaks in the day?

☐ Did I schedule my #1 most important thing?

EVENING REVIEW

Today was awesome because _____

_____

Today I struggled with _____

_____

On a scale of 1–10, with 10 being the highest, I would rate today's
productivity at a...   1 2 3 4 5 6 7 8 9 10

Tomorrow I will...   Other Thoughts/Notes

_____   _____

_____   _____

_____   _____

_____   _____

_____   _____

_____   _____

DAILY ACTION PLAN

Date: ___ / ___ / ___

S M T W Th F S

"Develop an attitude of gratitude.
Say thank you to everyone you meet for everything they do for you."
—BRIAN TRACY

MORNING ROUTINE

Wake-up time _____ Water ☐ Exercise ☐ Daily Journal ☐ _____ ☐

This morning, I'm grateful for _____

GOALS AND M.I.N.S.

Goals are important to review daily, reinforcing your objectives to your conscious and subconscious mind. But goals alone are not enough. It's also vital that you take time to identify your Most Important Next Step (M.I.N.S.) for each goal, so your goal transforms into an action. And remember, when it comes to M.I.N.S., be specific.

Real Estate Goal: _____

Weekly Objective: _____

M.I.N.S. _____

Second Goal: _____

Weekly Objective: _____

M.I.N.S. _____

Third Goal: _____

Weekly Objective: _____

M.I.N.S. _____

I can consider today a "win" if I _____

Now, go place this on your time-blocking calendar for today.

REAL ESTATE L.A.P.S. FUNNEL

Use this space to set a daily goal for defining how you'll get **leads**, how many properties you'll **analyze**, how many properties you'll **pursue** (offer), and how many you'll **purchase** today.

GOAL   REALITY

LEADS

ANALYZE

PURSUE

$

TODAY'S TIME-BLOCKING ACTIVITIES

High-achieving real estate investors know that what gets scheduled gets done.
Take a few minutes to think about your goals, your M.I.N.S., and schedule your day.
Don't forget to include several breaks.

5AM–6AM	_____	2PM–3PM _____
6AM–7AM	_____	3PM–4PM _____
7AM–8AM	_____	4PM–5PM _____
8AM–9AM	_____	5PM–6PM _____
9AM–10AM	_____	6PM–7PM _____
10AM–11AM	_____	7PM–8PM _____
11AM–12PM	_____	8PM–9PM _____
12PM–1PM	_____	9PM–10PM _____
1PM–2PM	_____	10PM–11PM _____

☐ Did I include enough breaks in the day?

☐ Did I schedule my #1 most important thing?

EVENING REVIEW

Today was awesome because _____

Today I struggled with _____

On a scale of 1–10, with 10 being the highest, I would rate today's productivity at a...   1   2   3   4   5   6   7   8   9   10

Tomorrow I will...

Other Thoughts/Notes

Date: ____ / ____ / ____   # DAILY ACTION PLAN   S M T W Th F S

"You cannot change your decision overnight,
but you can change your direction overnight."
—JIM ROHN

MORNING ROUTINE

Wake-up time _____   Water ☐   Exercise ☐   Daily Journal ☐   _____ ☐

This morning, I'm grateful for _____

GOALS AND M.I.N.S.

Goals are important to review daily, reinforcing your objectives to your conscious and
subconscious mind. But goals alone are not enough. It's also vital that you take time to
identify your Most Important Next Step (M.I.N.S.) for each goal, so your goal transforms
into an action. And remember, when it comes to M.I.N.S., be specific.

Real Estate Goal: _____

Weekly Objective: _____

M.I.N.S. _____

Second Goal: _____

Weekly Objective: _____

M.I.N.S. _____

Third Goal: _____

Weekly Objective: _____

M.I.N.S. _____

I can consider today a "win" if I _____

Now, go place this on your time-blocking calendar for today.

REAL ESTATE L.A.P.S. FUNNEL

Use this space to set a daily goal for
defining how you'll get **leads**, how many
properties you'll **analyze**, how many
properties you'll **pursue** (offer), and how
many you'll **purchase** today.

GOAL   REALITY

LEADS
ANALYZE
PURSUE
$

TODAY'S TIME-BLOCKING ACTIVITIES

High-achieving real estate investors know that what gets scheduled gets done.
Take a few minutes to think about your goals, your M.I.N.S., and schedule your day.
Don't forget to include several breaks.

5AM–6AM _____   2PM–3PM _____

6AM–7AM _____   3PM–4PM _____

7AM–8AM _____   4PM–5PM _____

8AM–9AM _____   5PM–6PM _____

9AM–10AM _____   6PM–7PM _____

10AM–11AM _____   7PM–8PM _____

11AM–12PM _____   8PM–9PM _____

12PM–1PM _____   9PM–10PM _____

1PM–2PM _____   10PM–11PM _____

☐ Did I include enough breaks   ☐ Did I schedule my #1 most
   in the day?   important thing?

EVENING REVIEW

Today was awesome because _____

_____

Today I struggled with _____

_____

On a scale of 1–10, with 10 being the highest, I would rate today's
productivity at a...   1 2 3 4 5 6 7 8 9 10

Tomorrow I will...   Other Thoughts/Notes

_____   _____

_____   _____

_____   _____

_____   _____

_____   _____

_____   _____

Date: _____ / _____ / _____ # DAILY ACTION PLAN

"In order to be irreplaceable one must always be different."
—Coco Chanel

MORNING ROUTINE

Wake-up time _____ Water ☐ Exercise ☐ Daily Journal ☐ _____ ☐

This morning, I'm grateful for _____

GOALS AND M.I.N.S.

Goals are important to review daily, reinforcing your objectives to your conscious and subconscious mind. But goals alone are not enough. It's also vital that you take time to identify your Most Important Next Step (M.I.N.S.) for each goal, so your goal transforms into an action. And remember, when it comes to M.I.N.S., be specific.

Real Estate Goal: _____

Weekly Objective: _____

M.I.N.S. _____

Second Goal: _____

Weekly Objective: _____

M.I.N.S. _____

Third Goal: _____

Weekly Objective: _____

M.I.N.S. _____

I can consider today a "win" if I _____

Now, go place this on your time-blocking calendar for today.

REAL ESTATE L.A.P.S. FUNNEL

Use this space to set a daily goal for defining how you'll get **leads**, how many properties you'll **analyze**, how many properties you'll **pursue** (offer), and how many you'll **purchase** today.

GOAL   REALITY

LEADS

ANALYZE

PURSUE

$

TODAY'S TIME-BLOCKING ACTIVITIES

High-achieving real estate investors know that what gets scheduled gets done.
Take a few minutes to think about your goals, your M.I.N.S., and schedule your day.
Don't forget to include several breaks.

5AM–6AM _____	2PM–3PM _____
6AM–7AM _____	3PM–4PM _____
7AM–8AM _____	4PM–5PM _____
8AM–9AM _____	5PM–6PM _____
9AM–10AM _____	6PM–7PM _____
10AM–11AM _____	7PM–8PM _____
11AM–12PM _____	8PM–9PM _____
12PM–1PM _____	9PM–10PM _____
1PM–2PM _____	10PM–11PM _____

☐ Did I include enough breaks in the day?

☐ Did I schedule my #1 most important thing?

EVENING REVIEW

Today was awesome because _____

_____

Today I struggled with _____

_____

On a scale of 1–10, with 10 being the highest, I would rate today's productivity at a...   1 2 3 4 5 6 7 8 9 10

Tomorrow I will...

Other Thoughts/Notes

DAILY ACTION PLAN

Date: ____ / ____ / ____

*"Entrepreneurial leadership requires the ability
to move quickly when opportunity presents itself."*
—Brian Tracy

MORNING ROUTINE

Wake-up time _____ Water ☐ Exercise ☐ Daily Journal ☐ _____ ☐

This morning, I'm grateful for _____

GOALS AND M.I.N.S.

Goals are important to review daily, reinforcing your objectives to your conscious and subconscious mind. But goals alone are not enough. It's also vital that you take time to identify your Most Important Next Step (M.I.N.S.) for each goal, so your goal transforms into an action. And remember, when it comes to M.I.N.S., be specific.

Real Estate Goal: _____

Weekly Objective: _____

M.I.N.S. _____

Second Goal: _____

Weekly Objective: _____

M.I.N.S. _____

Third Goal: _____

Weekly Objective: _____

M.I.N.S. _____

I can consider today a "win" if I _____

Now, go place this on your time-blocking calendar for today.

REAL ESTATE L.A.P.S. FUNNEL

Use this space to set a daily goal for defining how you'll get **leads**, how many properties you'll **analyze**, how many properties you'll **pursue** (offer), and how many you'll **purchase** today.

GOAL   REALITY

LEADS

ANALYZE

PURSUE

$

TODAY'S TIME-BLOCKING ACTIVITIES

High-achieving real estate investors know that what gets scheduled gets done.
Take a few minutes to think about your goals, your M.I.N.S., and schedule your day.
Don't forget to include several breaks.

5AM–6AM _____	2PM–3PM _____
6AM–7AM _____	3PM–4PM _____
7AM–8AM _____	4PM–5PM _____
8AM–9AM _____	5PM–6PM _____
9AM–10AM _____	6PM–7PM _____
10AM–11AM _____	7PM–8PM _____
11AM–12PM _____	8PM–9PM _____
12PM–1PM _____	9PM–10PM _____
1PM–2PM _____	10PM–11PM _____

☐ Did I include enough breaks in the day?

☐ Did I schedule my #1 most important thing?

EVENING REVIEW

Today was awesome because _____

_____

Today I struggled with _____

_____

On a scale of 1–10, with 10 being the highest, I would rate today's
productivity at a...   1 2 3 4 5 6 7 8 9 10

Tomorrow I will...   Other Thoughts/Notes

DAILY ACTION PLAN

Date: ___ / ___ / ___   S M T W Th F S

"Success is neither magical nor mysterious. Success is the natural consequence of consistently applying basic fundamentals."

—JIM ROHN

MORNING ROUTINE

Wake-up time _____ Water ☐ Exercise ☐ Daily Journal ☐ _____ ☐

This morning, I'm grateful for _____

GOALS AND M.I.N.S.

Goals are important to review daily, reinforcing your objectives to your conscious and subconscious mind. But goals alone are not enough. It's also vital that you take time to identify your Most Important Next Step (M.I.N.S.) for each goal, so your goal transforms into an action. And remember, when it comes to M.I.N.S., be specific.

Real Estate Goal: _____

Weekly Objective: _____

M.I.N.S. _____

Second Goal: _____

Weekly Objective: _____

M.I.N.S. _____

Third Goal: _____

Weekly Objective: _____

M.I.N.S. _____

I can consider today a "win" if I _____

Now, go place this on your time-blocking calendar for today.

REAL ESTATE L.A.P.S. FUNNEL

Use this space to set a daily goal for defining how you'll get **leads**, how many properties you'll **analyze**, how many properties you'll **pursue** (offer), and how many you'll **purchase** today.

GOAL   REALITY

LEADS

ANALYZE

PURSUE

$

TODAY'S TIME-BLOCKING ACTIVITIES

High-achieving real estate investors know that what gets scheduled gets done.
Take a few minutes to think about your goals, your M.I.N.S., and schedule your day.
Don't forget to include several breaks.

5AM–6AM _____	2PM–3PM _____
6AM–7AM _____	3PM–4PM _____
7AM–8AM _____	4PM–5PM _____
8AM–9AM _____	5PM–6PM _____
9AM–10AM _____	6PM–7PM _____
10AM–11AM _____	7PM–8PM _____
11AM–12PM _____	8PM–9PM _____
12PM–1PM _____	9PM–10PM _____
1PM–2PM _____	10PM–11PM _____

☐ Did I include enough breaks in the day?

☐ Did I schedule my #1 most important thing?

EVENING REVIEW

Today was awesome because _____

_____

Today I struggled with _____

_____

On a scale of 1–10, with 10 being the highest, I would rate today's
productivity at a...   1   2   3   4   5   6   7   8   9   10

Tomorrow I will...   Other Thoughts/Notes

_____   _____

_____   _____

_____   _____

_____   _____

_____   _____

_____   _____

DAILY ACTION PLAN

"Only I can change my life. No one can do it for me."
—Carol Burnett

MORNING ROUTINE

Wake-up time _____ Water ☐ Exercise ☐ Daily Journal ☐ _____ ☐

This morning, I'm grateful for _____

GOALS AND M.I.N.S.

Goals are important to review daily, reinforcing your objectives to your conscious and subconscious mind. But goals alone are not enough. It's also vital that you take time to identify your Most Important Next Step (M.I.N.S.) for each goal, so your goal transforms into an action. And remember, when it comes to M.I.N.S., be specific.

Real Estate Goal: _____

Weekly Objective: _____

M.I.N.S. _____

Second Goal: _____

Weekly Objective: _____

M.I.N.S. _____

Third Goal: _____

Weekly Objective: _____

M.I.N.S. _____

I can consider today a "win" if I _____

Now, go place this on your time-blocking calendar for today.

REAL ESTATE L.A.P.S. FUNNEL

Use this space to set a daily goal for defining how you'll get **leads**, how many properties you'll **analyze**, how many properties you'll **pursue** (offer), and how many you'll **purchase** today.

GOAL   REALITY

LEADS

ANALYZE

PURSUE

$

TODAY'S TIME-BLOCKING ACTIVITIES

High-achieving real estate investors know that what gets scheduled gets done.
Take a few minutes to think about your goals, your M.I.N.S., and schedule your day.
Don't forget to include several breaks.

5AM–6AM _____   2PM–3PM _____

6AM–7AM _____   3PM–4PM _____

7AM–8AM _____   4PM–5PM _____

8AM–9AM _____   5PM–6PM _____

9AM–10AM _____   6PM–7PM _____

10AM–11AM _____   7PM–8PM _____

11AM–12PM _____   8PM–9PM _____

12PM–1PM _____   9PM–10PM _____

1PM–2PM _____   10PM–11PM _____

☐ Did I include enough breaks   ☐ Did I schedule my #1 most
   in the day?   important thing?

EVENING REVIEW

Today was awesome because _____

_____

Today I struggled with _____

_____

On a scale of 1–10, with 10 being the highest, I would rate today's
productivity at a...   1 2 3 4 5 6 7 8 9 10

Tomorrow I will...   Other Thoughts/Notes

Date: ___ / ___ / ___   # DAILY ACTION PLAN   S M T W Th F S

MORNING ROUTINE

Wake-up time _____ Water ☐ Exercise ☐ Daily Journal ☐ _____ ☐

This morning, I'm grateful for _____

GOALS AND M.I.N.S.

*Goals are important to review daily, reinforcing your objectives to your conscious and
subconscious mind. But goals alone are not enough. It's also vital that you take time to
identify your Most Important Next Step (M.I.N.S.) for each goal, so your goal transforms
into an action. And remember, when it comes to M.I.N.S., be specific.*

Real Estate Goal: _____

Weekly Objective: _____

M.I.N.S. _____

Second Goal: _____

Weekly Objective: _____

M.I.N.S. _____

Third Goal: _____

Weekly Objective: _____

M.I.N.S. _____

I can consider today a "win" if I _____

Now, go place this on your time-blocking calendar for today.

REAL ESTATE L.A.P.S. FUNNEL

GOAL   REALITY

Use this space to set a daily goal for
defining how you'll get **leads**, how many
properties you'll **analyze**, how many
properties you'll **pursue** (offer), and how
many you'll **purchase** today.

LEADS

ANALYZE

PURSUE

$

TODAY'S TIME-BLOCKING ACTIVITIES

High-achieving real estate investors know that what gets scheduled gets done.
Take a few minutes to think about your goals, your M.I.N.S., and schedule your day.
Don't forget to include several breaks.

5AM–6AM _____   2PM–3PM _____

6AM–7AM _____   3PM–4PM _____

7AM–8AM _____   4PM–5PM _____

8AM–9AM _____   5PM–6PM _____

9AM–10AM _____   6PM–7PM _____

10AM–11AM _____   7PM–8PM _____

11AM–12PM _____   8PM–9PM _____

12PM–1PM _____   9PM–10PM _____

1PM–2PM _____   10PM–11PM _____

☐ Did I include enough breaks in the day?   ☐ Did I schedule my #1 most important thing?

EVENING REVIEW

Today was awesome because _____

_____

Today I struggled with _____

_____

On a scale of 1–10, with 10 being the highest, I would rate today's
productivity at a...   1 2 3 4 5 6 7 8 9 10

Tomorrow I will...   Other Thoughts/Notes

_____   _____

_____   _____

_____   _____

_____   _____

_____   _____

_____   _____

DAILY ACTION PLAN

Date: ___ / ___ / ___

S M T W Th F S

*"Optimism is the faith that leads to achievement.
Nothing can be done without hope and confidence."*
—HELEN KELLER

MORNING ROUTINE

Wake-up time _____ Water ☐ Exercise ☐ Daily Journal ☐ _____ ☐

This morning, I'm grateful for _____

GOALS AND M.I.N.S.

Goals are important to review daily, reinforcing your objectives to your conscious and subconscious mind. But goals alone are not enough. It's also vital that you take time to identify your Most Important Next Step (M.I.N.S.) for each goal, so your goal transforms into an action. And remember, when it comes to M.I.N.S., be specific.

Real Estate Goal: _____

Weekly Objective: _____

M.I.N.S. _____

Second Goal: _____

Weekly Objective: _____

M.I.N.S. _____

Third Goal: _____

Weekly Objective: _____

M.I.N.S. _____

I can consider today a "win" if I _____

Now, go place this on your time-blocking calendar for today.

REAL ESTATE L.A.P.S. FUNNEL

Use this space to set a daily goal for defining how you'll get **leads**, how many properties you'll **analyze**, how many properties you'll **pursue** (offer), and how many you'll **purchase** today.

GOAL   REALITY

LEADS

ANALYZE

PURSUE

$

TODAY'S TIME-BLOCKING ACTIVITIES

High-achieving real estate investors know that what gets scheduled gets done.
Take a few minutes to think about your goals, your M.I.N.S., and schedule your day.
Don't forget to include several breaks.

5AM–6AM _____	2PM–3PM _____
6AM–7AM _____	3PM–4PM _____
7AM–8AM _____	4PM–5PM _____
8AM–9AM _____	5PM–6PM _____
9AM–10AM _____	6PM–7PM _____
10AM–11AM _____	7PM–8PM _____
11AM–12PM _____	8PM–9PM _____
12PM–1PM _____	9PM–10PM _____
1PM–2PM _____	10PM–11PM _____

☐ Did I include enough breaks in the day?

☐ Did I schedule my #1 most important thing?

EVENING REVIEW

Today was awesome because _____
_____

Today I struggled with _____
_____

On a scale of 1–10, with 10 being the highest, I would rate today's productivity at a...   1   2   3   4   5   6   7   8   9   10

Tomorrow I will...

Other Thoughts/Notes

Date: ____ / ____ / ____   # DAILY ACTION PLAN   S M T W Th F S

"Good, better, best. Never let it rest.
'Til your good is better and your better is best."
—St. Jerome

MORNING ROUTINE

Wake-up time _____   Water ☐   Exercise ☐   Daily Journal ☐   _____ ☐

This morning, I'm grateful for _____

GOALS AND M.I.N.S.

Goals are important to review daily, reinforcing your objectives to your conscious and subconscious mind. But goals alone are not enough. It's also vital that you take time to identify your Most Important Next Step (M.I.N.S.) for each goal, so your goal transforms into an action. And remember, when it comes to M.I.N.S., be specific.

Real Estate Goal: _____

Weekly Objective: _____

M.I.N.S. _____

Second Goal: _____

Weekly Objective: _____

M.I.N.S. _____

Third Goal: _____

Weekly Objective: _____

M.I.N.S. _____

I can consider today a "win" if I _____

Now, go place this on your time-blocking calendar for today.

REAL ESTATE L.A.P.S. FUNNEL

GOAL   REALITY

Use this space to set a daily goal for defining how you'll get **leads**, how many properties you'll **analyze**, how many properties you'll **pursue** (offer), and how many you'll **purchase** today.

LEADS

ANALYZE

PURSUE

$

TODAY'S TIME-BLOCKING ACTIVITIES

High-achieving real estate investors know that what gets scheduled gets done.
Take a few minutes to think about your goals, your M.I.N.S., and schedule your day.
Don't forget to include several breaks.

5AM–6AM _____	2PM–3PM _____
6AM–7AM _____	3PM–4PM _____
7AM–8AM _____	4PM–5PM _____
8AM–9AM _____	5PM–6PM _____
9AM–10AM _____	6PM–7PM _____
10AM–11AM _____	7PM–8PM _____
11AM–12PM _____	8PM–9PM _____
12PM–1PM _____	9PM–10PM _____
1PM–2PM _____	10PM–11PM _____

☐ Did I include enough breaks in the day?

☐ Did I schedule my #1 most important thing?

EVENING REVIEW

Today was awesome because _____

_____

Today I struggled with _____

_____

On a scale of 1–10, with 10 being the highest, I would rate today's
productivity at a...   1   2   3   4   5   6   7   8   9   10

Tomorrow I will...   Other Thoughts/Notes

DAILY ACTION PLAN

Date: _____ / _____ / _____   S M T W Th F S

"With the new day comes new strength and new thoughts."
—ELEANOR ROOSEVELT

MORNING ROUTINE

Wake-up time _____   Water ☐   Exercise ☐   Daily Journal ☐   _____ ☐

This morning, I'm grateful for _____

GOALS AND M.I.N.S.

Goals are important to review daily, reinforcing your objectives to your conscious and subconscious mind. But goals alone are not enough. It's also vital that you take time to identify your Most Important Next Step (M.I.N.S.) for each goal, so your goal transforms into an action. And remember, when it comes to M.I.N.S., be specific.

Real Estate Goal: _____

Weekly Objective: _____

M.I.N.S. _____

Second Goal: _____

Weekly Objective: _____

M.I.N.S. _____

Third Goal: _____

Weekly Objective: _____

M.I.N.S. _____

I can consider today a "win" if I _____

Now, go place this on your time-blocking calendar for today.

REAL ESTATE L.A.P.S. FUNNEL

Use this space to set a daily goal for defining how you'll get **leads**, how many properties you'll **analyze**, how many properties you'll **pursue** (offer), and how many you'll **purchase** today.

GOAL   REALITY

LEADS

ANALYZE

PURSUE

$

TODAY'S TIME-BLOCKING ACTIVITIES

High-achieving real estate investors know that what gets scheduled gets done.
Take a few minutes to think about your goals, your M.I.N.S., and schedule your day.
Don't forget to include several breaks.

5AM–6AM _____   2PM–3PM _____

6AM–7AM _____   3PM–4PM _____

7AM–8AM _____   4PM–5PM _____

8AM–9AM _____   5PM–6PM _____

9AM–10AM _____   6PM–7PM _____

10AM–11AM _____   7PM–8PM _____

11AM–12PM _____   8PM–9PM _____

12PM–1PM _____   9PM–10PM _____

1PM–2PM _____   10PM–11PM _____

☐ Did I include enough breaks
   in the day?

☐ Did I schedule my #1 most
   important thing?

EVENING REVIEW

Today was awesome because _____

_____

Today I struggled with _____

_____

On a scale of 1–10, with 10 being the highest, I would rate today's
productivity at a...   1 2 3 4 5 6 7 8 9 10

Tomorrow I will...   Other Thoughts/Notes

_____   _____

_____   _____

_____   _____

_____   _____

_____   _____

_____   _____

DAILY ACTION PLAN

Date: ____ / ____ / ____   S M T W Th F S

"You will never win if you never begin."
—Helen Rowland

MORNING ROUTINE

Wake-up time _____ Water ☐ Exercise ☐ Daily Journal ☐ _____ ☐

This morning, I'm grateful for _____

GOALS AND M.I.N.S.

Goals are important to review daily, reinforcing your objectives to your conscious and subconscious mind. But goals alone are not enough. It's also vital that you take time to identify your Most Important Next Step (M.I.N.S.) for each goal, so your goal transforms into an action. And remember, when it comes to M.I.N.S., be specific.

Real Estate Goal: _____

Weekly Objective: _____

M.I.N.S. _____

Second Goal: _____

Weekly Objective: _____

M.I.N.S. _____

Third Goal: _____

Weekly Objective: _____

M.I.N.S. _____

I can consider today a "win" if I _____

Now, go place this on your time-blocking calendar for today.

REAL ESTATE L.A.P.S. FUNNEL

Use this space to set a daily goal for defining how you'll get **leads**, how many properties you'll **analyze**, how many properties you'll **pursue** (offer), and how many you'll **purchase** today.

GOAL   REALITY

LEADS

ANALYZE

PURSUE

$

TODAY'S TIME-BLOCKING ACTIVITIES

High-achieving real estate investors know that what gets scheduled gets done.
Take a few minutes to think about your goals, your M.I.N.S., and schedule your day.
Don't forget to include several breaks.

5AM–6AM _____	2PM–3PM _____
6AM–7AM _____	3PM–4PM _____
7AM–8AM _____	4PM–5PM _____
8AM–9AM _____	5PM–6PM _____
9AM–10AM _____	6PM–7PM _____
10AM–11AM _____	7PM–8PM _____
11AM–12PM _____	8PM–9PM _____
12PM–1PM _____	9PM–10PM _____
1PM–2PM _____	10PM–11PM _____

☐ Did I include enough breaks in the day?

☐ Did I schedule my #1 most important thing?

EVENING REVIEW

Today was awesome because _____

_____

Today I struggled with _____

_____

On a scale of 1–10, with 10 being the highest, I would rate today's
productivity at a...   1   2   3   4   5   6   7   8   9   10

Tomorrow I will...   Other Thoughts/Notes

DAILY ACTION PLAN

Date: ____ / ____ / ____

S M T W Th F S

"The past cannot be changed. The future is yet in your power."
—MARY PICKFORD

MORNING ROUTINE

Wake-up time _____ Water ☐ Exercise ☐ Daily Journal ☐ _____ ☐

This morning, I'm grateful for _____

GOALS AND M.I.N.S.

Goals are important to review daily, reinforcing your objectives to your conscious and subconscious mind. But goals alone are not enough. It's also vital that you take time to identify your Most Important Next Step (M.I.N.S.) for each goal, so your goal transforms into an action. And remember, when it comes to M.I.N.S., be specific.

Real Estate Goal: _____

Weekly Objective: _____

M.I.N.S. _____

Second Goal: _____

Weekly Objective: _____

M.I.N.S. _____

Third Goal: _____

Weekly Objective: _____

M.I.N.S. _____

I can consider today a "win" if I _____

Now, go place this on your time-blocking calendar for today.

REAL ESTATE L.A.P.S. FUNNEL

Use this space to set a daily goal for defining how you'll get **leads**, how many properties you'll **analyze**, how many properties you'll **pursue** (offer), and how many you'll **purchase** today.

GOAL

REALITY

LEADS

ANALYZE

PURSUE

$

TODAY'S TIME-BLOCKING ACTIVITIES

High-achieving real estate investors know that what gets scheduled gets done.
Take a few minutes to think about your goals, your M.I.N.S., and schedule your day.
Don't forget to include several breaks.

5AM–6AM	_____	2PM–3PM	_____
6AM–7AM	_____	3PM–4PM	_____
7AM–8AM	_____	4PM–5PM	_____
8AM–9AM	_____	5PM–6PM	_____
9AM–10AM	_____	6PM–7PM	_____
10AM–11AM	_____	7PM–8PM	_____
11AM–12PM	_____	8PM–9PM	_____
12PM–1PM	_____	9PM–10PM	_____
1PM–2PM	_____	10PM–11PM	_____

☐ Did I include enough breaks in the day?

☐ Did I schedule my #1 most important thing?

EVENING REVIEW

Today was awesome because _____

_____

Today I struggled with _____

_____

On a scale of 1–10, with 10 being the highest, I would rate today's productivity at a...   1 2 3 4 5 6 7 8 9 10

Tomorrow I will...

Other Thoughts/Notes

Date: ____ / ____ / ____   # DAILY ACTION PLAN

"Always do your best. What you plant now, you will harvest later."
—Og Mandino

MORNING ROUTINE

Wake-up time _____   Water ☐   Exercise ☐   Daily Journal ☐   _____ ☐

This morning, I'm grateful for _____

GOALS AND M.I.N.S.

Goals are important to review daily, reinforcing your objectives to your conscious and subconscious mind. But goals alone are not enough. It's also vital that you take time to identify your Most Important Next Step (M.I.N.S.) for each goal, so your goal transforms into an action. And remember, when it comes to M.I.N.S., be specific.

Real Estate Goal: _____

Weekly Objective: _____

M.I.N.S. _____

Second Goal: _____

Weekly Objective: _____

M.I.N.S. _____

Third Goal: _____

Weekly Objective: _____

M.I.N.S. _____

I can consider today a "win" if I _____

Now, go place this on your time-blocking calendar for today.

REAL ESTATE L.A.P.S. FUNNEL

Use this space to set a daily goal for defining how you'll get **leads**, how many properties you'll **analyze**, how many properties you'll **pursue** (offer), and how many you'll **purchase** today.

GOAL   REALITY

LEADS

ANALYZE

PURSUE

$

TODAY'S TIME-BLOCKING ACTIVITIES

High-achieving real estate investors know that what gets scheduled gets done.
Take a few minutes to think about your goals, your M.I.N.S., and schedule your day.
Don't forget to include several breaks.

5AM–6AM _____	2PM–3PM _____
6AM–7AM _____	3PM–4PM _____
7AM–8AM _____	4PM–5PM _____
8AM–9AM _____	5PM–6PM _____
9AM–10AM _____	6PM–7PM _____
10AM–11AM _____	7PM–8PM _____
11AM–12PM _____	8PM–9PM _____
12PM–1PM _____	9PM–10PM _____
1PM–2PM _____	10PM–11PM _____

☐ Did I include enough breaks in the day?

☐ Did I schedule my #1 most important thing?

EVENING REVIEW

Today was awesome because _____

_____

Today I struggled with _____

_____

On a scale of 1–10, with 10 being the highest, I would rate today's
productivity at a...   1 2 3 4 5 6 7 8 9 10

Tomorrow I will...

_____

_____

_____

_____

_____

Other Thoughts/Notes

_____

_____

_____

_____

_____

DAILY ACTION PLAN

Date: ____ / ____ / ____   S M T W Th F S

MORNING ROUTINE

Wake-up time _____   Water ☐   Exercise ☐   Daily Journal ☐   _____ ☐

This morning, I'm grateful for _____

GOALS AND M.I.N.S.

Goals are important to review daily, reinforcing your objectives to your conscious and subconscious mind. But goals alone are not enough. It's also vital that you take time to identify your Most Important Next Step (M.I.N.S.) for each goal, so your goal transforms into an action. And remember, when it comes to M.I.N.S., be specific.

Real Estate Goal: _____

Weekly Objective: _____

M.I.N.S. _____

Second Goal: _____

Weekly Objective: _____

M.I.N.S. _____

Third Goal: _____

Weekly Objective: _____

M.I.N.S. _____

I can consider today a "win" if I _____

Now, go place this on your time-blocking calendar for today.

REAL ESTATE L.A.P.S. FUNNEL

Use this space to set a daily goal for defining how you'll get **leads**, how many properties you'll **analyze**, how many properties you'll **pursue** (offer), and how many you'll **purchase** today.

GOAL   REALITY

LEADS

ANALYZE

PURSUE

$

TODAY'S TIME-BLOCKING ACTIVITIES

High-achieving real estate investors know that what gets scheduled gets done.
Take a few minutes to think about your goals, your M.I.N.S., and schedule your day.
Don't forget to include several breaks.

5AM–6AM _____   2PM–3PM _____

6AM–7AM _____   3PM–4PM _____

7AM–8AM _____   4PM–5PM _____

8AM–9AM _____   5PM–6PM _____

9AM–10AM _____   6PM–7PM _____

10AM–11AM _____   7PM–8PM _____

11AM–12PM _____   8PM–9PM _____

12PM–1PM _____   9PM–10PM _____

1PM–2PM _____   10PM–11PM _____

☐ Did I include enough breaks   ☐ Did I schedule my #1 most
in the day?   important thing?

EVENING REVIEW

Today was awesome because _____

_____

Today I struggled with _____

_____

On a scale of 1–10, with 10 being the highest, I would rate today's
productivity at a... 1 2 3 4 5 6 7 8 9 10

Tomorrow I will...   Other Thoughts/Notes

_____   _____

_____   _____

_____   _____

_____   _____

_____   _____

DAILY ACTION PLAN

Date: ____ / ____ / ____

S M T W Th F S

"I choose to make the rest of my life the best of my life."
—Louise Hay

MORNING ROUTINE

Wake-up time _____ Water ☐ Exercise ☐ Daily Journal ☐ _____ ☐

This morning, I'm grateful for _____

GOALS AND M.I.N.S.

Goals are important to review daily, reinforcing your objectives to your conscious and subconscious mind. But goals alone are not enough. It's also vital that you take time to identify your Most Important Next Step (M.I.N.S.) for each goal, so your goal transforms into an action. And remember, when it comes to M.I.N.S., be specific.

Real Estate Goal: _____

Weekly Objective: _____

M.I.N.S. _____

Second Goal: _____

Weekly Objective: _____

M.I.N.S. _____

Third Goal: _____

Weekly Objective: _____

M.I.N.S. _____

I can consider today a "win" if I _____

Now, go place this on your time-blocking calendar for today.

REAL ESTATE L.A.P.S. FUNNEL

Use this space to set a daily goal for defining how you'll get **leads**, how many properties you'll **analyze**, how many properties you'll **pursue** (offer), and how many you'll **purchase** today.

GOAL   REALITY

LEADS

ANALYZE

PURSUE

$

TODAY'S TIME-BLOCKING ACTIVITIES

High-achieving real estate investors know that what gets scheduled gets done.
Take a few minutes to think about your goals, your M.I.N.S., and schedule your day.
Don't forget to include several breaks.

5AM–6AM	_____	2PM–3PM	_____
6AM–7AM	_____	3PM–4PM	_____
7AM–8AM	_____	4PM–5PM	_____
8AM–9AM	_____	5PM–6PM	_____
9AM–10AM	_____	6PM–7PM	_____
10AM–11AM	_____	7PM–8PM	_____
11AM–12PM	_____	8PM–9PM	_____
12PM–1PM	_____	9PM–10PM	_____
1PM–2PM	_____	10PM–11PM	_____

☐ Did I include enough breaks in the day?

☐ Did I schedule my #1 most important thing?

EVENING REVIEW

Today was awesome because _____

_____

Today I struggled with _____

_____

On a scale of 1–10, with 10 being the highest, I would rate today's
productivity at a...   1   2   3   4   5   6   7   8   9   10

Tomorrow I will...

Other Thoughts/Notes

Date: ___ /___ /___   # DAILY ACTION PLAN   S M T W Th F S

MORNING ROUTINE

Wake-up time _____ Water ☐ Exercise ☐ Daily Journal ☐ _____ ☐

This morning, I'm grateful for _____

GOALS AND M.I.N.S.

*Goals are important to review daily, reinforcing your objectives to your conscious and
subconscious mind. But goals alone are not enough. It's also vital that you take time to
identify your Most Important Next Step (M.I.N.S.) for each goal, so your goal transforms
into an action. And remember, when it comes to M.I.N.S., be specific.*

Real Estate Goal: _____

Weekly Objective: _____

M.I.N.S. _____

Second Goal: _____

Weekly Objective: _____

M.I.N.S. _____

Third Goal: _____

Weekly Objective: _____

M.I.N.S. _____

I can consider today a "win" if I _____

Now, go place this on your time-blocking calendar for today.

REAL ESTATE L.A.P.S. FUNNEL

Use this space to set a daily goal for
defining how you'll get **leads**, how many
properties you'll **analyze**, how many
properties you'll **pursue** (offer), and how
many you'll **purchase** today.

GOAL   REALITY

LEADS

ANALYZE

PURSUE

$

TODAY'S TIME-BLOCKING ACTIVITIES

High-achieving real estate investors know that what gets scheduled gets done.
Take a few minutes to think about your goals, your M.I.N.S., and schedule your day.
Don't forget to include several breaks.

5AM–6AM _____   2PM–3PM _____

6AM–7AM _____   3PM–4PM _____

7AM–8AM _____   4PM–5PM _____

8AM–9AM _____   5PM–6PM _____

9AM–10AM _____   6PM–7PM _____

10AM–11AM _____   7PM–8PM _____

11AM–12PM _____   8PM–9PM _____

12PM–1PM _____   9PM–10PM _____

1PM–2PM _____   10PM–11PM _____

☐ Did I include enough breaks in the day?   ☐ Did I schedule my #1 most important thing?

EVENING REVIEW

Today was awesome because _____

_____

Today I struggled with _____

_____

On a scale of 1–10, with 10 being the highest, I would rate today's
productivity at a...   1 2 3 4 5 6 7 8 9 10

Tomorrow I will...   Other Thoughts/Notes

_____   _____

_____   _____

_____   _____

_____   _____

_____   _____

_____   _____

DAILY ACTION PLAN

Date: ___ / ___ / ___

"It always seems impossible until it's done."
—NELSON MANDELA

MORNING ROUTINE

Wake-up time _____ Water ☐ Exercise ☐ Daily Journal ☐ _____ ☐

This morning, I'm grateful for _____

GOALS AND M.I.N.S.

Goals are important to review daily, reinforcing your objectives to your conscious and subconscious mind. But goals alone are not enough. It's also vital that you take time to identify your Most Important Next Step (M.I.N.S.) for each goal, so your goal transforms into an action. And remember, when it comes to M.I.N.S., be specific.

Real Estate Goal: _____

Weekly Objective: _____

M.I.N.S. _____

Second Goal: _____

Weekly Objective: _____

M.I.N.S. _____

Third Goal: _____

Weekly Objective: _____

M.I.N.S. _____

I can consider today a "win" if I _____

Now, go place this on your time-blocking calendar for today.

REAL ESTATE L.A.P.S. FUNNEL

Use this space to set a daily goal for defining how you'll get **leads**, how many properties you'll **analyze**, how many properties you'll **pursue** (offer), and how many you'll **purchase** today.

GOAL   REALITY

LEADS

ANALYZE

PURSUE

$

TODAY'S TIME-BLOCKING ACTIVITIES

High-achieving real estate investors know that what gets scheduled gets done.
Take a few minutes to think about your goals, your M.I.N.S., and schedule your day.
Don't forget to include several breaks.

5AM–6AM _____	2PM–3PM _____
6AM–7AM _____	3PM–4PM _____
7AM–8AM _____	4PM–5PM _____
8AM–9AM _____	5PM–6PM _____
9AM–10AM _____	6PM–7PM _____
10AM–11AM _____	7PM–8PM _____
11AM–12PM _____	8PM–9PM _____
12PM–1PM _____	9PM–10PM _____
1PM–2PM _____	10PM–11PM _____

☐ Did I include enough breaks in the day?

☐ Did I schedule my #1 most important thing?

EVENING REVIEW

Today was awesome because _____

_____

Today I struggled with _____

_____

On a scale of 1–10, with 10 being the highest, I would rate today's
productivity at a...   1 2 3 4 5 6 7 8 9 10

Tomorrow I will...

Other Thoughts/Notes

DAILY ACTION PLAN

Date: ____ / ____ / ____

"Believe in yourself! Have faith in your abilities! Without a humble but reasonable confidence in your own powers you cannot be successful or happy."
—Norman Vincent Peale

MORNING ROUTINE

Wake-up time _____ Water ☐ Exercise ☐ Daily Journal ☐ _____ ☐

This morning, I'm grateful for _____

GOALS AND M.I.N.S.

Goals are important to review daily, reinforcing your objectives to your conscious and subconscious mind. But goals alone are not enough. It's also vital that you take time to identify your Most Important Next Step (M.I.N.S.) for each goal, so your goal transforms into an action. And remember, when it comes to M.I.N.S., be specific.

Real Estate Goal: _____

Weekly Objective: _____

M.I.N.S. _____

Second Goal: _____

Weekly Objective: _____

M.I.N.S. _____

Third Goal: _____

Weekly Objective: _____

M.I.N.S. _____

I can consider today a "win" if I _____

Now, go place this on your time-blocking calendar for today.

REAL ESTATE L.A.P.S. FUNNEL

Use this space to set a daily goal for defining how you'll get **leads**, how many properties you'll **analyze**, how many properties you'll **pursue** (offer), and how many you'll **purchase** today.

GOAL   REALITY

LEADS

ANALYZE

PURSUE

$

TODAY'S TIME-BLOCKING ACTIVITIES

High-achieving real estate investors know that what gets scheduled gets done.
Take a few minutes to think about your goals, your M.I.N.S., and schedule your day.
Don't forget to include several breaks.

5AM–6AM	_____	2PM–3PM	_____
6AM–7AM	_____	3PM–4PM	_____
7AM–8AM	_____	4PM–5PM	_____
8AM–9AM	_____	5PM–6PM	_____
9AM–10AM	_____	6PM–7PM	_____
10AM–11AM	_____	7PM–8PM	_____
11AM–12PM	_____	8PM–9PM	_____
12PM–1PM	_____	9PM–10PM	_____
1PM–2PM	_____	10PM–11PM	_____

☐ Did I include enough breaks in the day?

☐ Did I schedule my #1 most important thing?

EVENING REVIEW

Today was awesome because _____

_____

Today I struggled with _____

_____

On a scale of 1–10, with 10 being the highest, I would rate today's
productivity at a...   1 2 3 4 5 6 7 8 9 10

Tomorrow I will...

Other Thoughts/Notes

DAILY ACTION PLAN

Date: ____ / ____ / ____

S M T W Th F S

"It does not matter how slowly you go as long as you do not stop."
—CONFUCIUS

MORNING ROUTINE

Wake-up time _____ Water ☐ Exercise ☐ Daily Journal ☐ _____ ☐

This morning, I'm grateful for _____

GOALS AND M.I.N.S.

Goals are important to review daily, reinforcing your objectives to your conscious and subconscious mind. But goals alone are not enough. It's also vital that you take time to identify your Most Important Next Step (M.I.N.S.) for each goal, so your goal transforms into an action. And remember, when it comes to M.I.N.S., be specific.

Real Estate Goal: _____

Weekly Objective: _____

M.I.N.S. _____

Second Goal: _____

Weekly Objective: _____

M.I.N.S. _____

Third Goal: _____

Weekly Objective: _____

M.I.N.S. _____

I can consider today a "win" if I _____

Now, go place this on your time-blocking calendar for today.

REAL ESTATE L.A.P.S. FUNNEL

Use this space to set a daily goal for defining how you'll get **leads**, how many properties you'll **analyze**, how many properties you'll **pursue** (offer), and how many you'll **purchase** today.

GOAL   REALITY

LEADS

ANALYZE

PURSUE

$

TODAY'S TIME-BLOCKING ACTIVITIES

High-achieving real estate investors know that what gets scheduled gets done.
Take a few minutes to think about your goals, your M.I.N.S., and schedule your day.
Don't forget to include several breaks.

5AM–6AM _____   2PM–3PM _____

6AM–7AM _____   3PM–4PM _____

7AM–8AM _____   4PM–5PM _____

8AM–9AM _____   5PM–6PM _____

9AM–10AM _____   6PM–7PM _____

10AM–11AM _____   7PM–8PM _____

11AM–12PM _____   8PM–9PM _____

12PM–1PM _____   9PM–10PM _____

1PM–2PM _____   10PM–11PM _____

☐ Did I include enough breaks in the day?   ☐ Did I schedule my #1 most important thing?

EVENING REVIEW

Today was awesome because _____

_____

Today I struggled with _____

_____

On a scale of 1–10, with 10 being the highest, I would rate today's productivity at a...   1 2 3 4 5 6 7 8 9 10

Tomorrow I will...   Other Thoughts/Notes

_____   _____

_____   _____

_____   _____

_____   _____

_____   _____

_____   _____

DAILY ACTION PLAN

Date: ____ / ____ / ____   S M T W Th F S

"Failure will never take me if my determination
to succeed is strong enough."
—Og Mandino

MORNING ROUTINE

Wake-up time _____   Water ☐   Exercise ☐   Daily Journal ☐   _____ ☐

This morning, I'm grateful for _____

GOALS AND M.I.N.S.

Goals are important to review daily, reinforcing your objectives to your conscious and subconscious mind. But goals alone are not enough. It's also vital that you take time to identify your Most Important Next Step (M.I.N.S.) for each goal, so your goal transforms into an action. And remember, when it comes to M.I.N.S., be specific.

Real Estate Goal: _____

Weekly Objective: _____

M.I.N.S. _____

Second Goal: _____

Weekly Objective: _____

M.I.N.S. _____

Third Goal: _____

Weekly Objective: _____

M.I.N.S. _____

I can consider today a "win" if I _____

Now, go place this on your time-blocking calendar for today.

REAL ESTATE L.A.P.S. FUNNEL

Use this space to set a daily goal for defining how you'll get **leads**, how many properties you'll **analyze**, how many properties you'll **pursue** (offer), and how many you'll **purchase** today.

GOAL   REALITY

LEADS

ANALYZE

PURSUE

$

TODAY'S TIME-BLOCKING ACTIVITIES

High-achieving real estate investors know that what gets scheduled gets done.
Take a few minutes to think about your goals, your M.I.N.S., and schedule your day.
Don't forget to include several breaks.

5AM–6AM _____	2PM–3PM _____
6AM–7AM _____	3PM–4PM _____
7AM–8AM _____	4PM–5PM _____
8AM–9AM _____	5PM–6PM _____
9AM–10AM _____	6PM–7PM _____
10AM–11AM _____	7PM–8PM _____
11AM–12PM _____	8PM–9PM _____
12PM–1PM _____	9PM–10PM _____
1PM–2PM _____	10PM–11PM _____

☐ Did I include enough breaks in the day?

☐ Did I schedule my #1 most important thing?

EVENING REVIEW

Today was awesome because _____

_____

Today I struggled with _____

_____

On a scale of 1–10, with 10 being the highest, I would rate today's
productivity at a...   1 2 3 4 5 6 7 8 9 10

Tomorrow I will...   Other Thoughts/Notes

DAILY ACTION PLAN

Date: ____ / ____ / ____   S M T W Th F S

*"Setting goals is the first step in turning
the invisible into the visible."*
—TONY ROBBINS

MORNING ROUTINE

Wake-up time _____   Water ☐   Exercise ☐   Daily Journal ☐   _____ ☐

This morning, I'm grateful for _____

GOALS AND M.I.N.S.

*Goals are important to review daily, reinforcing your objectives to your conscious and
subconscious mind. But goals alone are not enough. It's also vital that you take time to
identify your Most Important Next Step (M.I.N.S.) for each goal, so your goal transforms
into an action. And remember, when it comes to M.I.N.S., be specific.*

Real Estate Goal: _____

Weekly Objective: _____

M.I.N.S. _____

Second Goal: _____

Weekly Objective: _____

M.I.N.S. _____

Third Goal: _____

Weekly Objective: _____

M.I.N.S. _____

I can consider today a "win" if I _____

Now, go place this on your time-blocking calendar for today.

REAL ESTATE L.A.P.S. FUNNEL

Use this space to set a daily goal for
defining how you'll get **leads**, how many
properties you'll **analyze**, how many
properties you'll **pursue** (offer), and how
many you'll **purchase** today.

GOAL   REALITY

LEADS

ANALYZE

PURSUE

$

TODAY'S TIME-BLOCKING ACTIVITIES

High-achieving real estate investors know that what gets scheduled gets done.
Take a few minutes to think about your goals, your M.I.N.S., and schedule your day.
Don't forget to include several breaks.

5AM–6AM _____   2PM–3PM _____

6AM–7AM _____   3PM–4PM _____

7AM–8AM _____   4PM–5PM _____

8AM–9AM _____   5PM–6PM _____

9AM–10AM _____   6PM–7PM _____

10AM–11AM _____   7PM–8PM _____

11AM–12PM _____   8PM–9PM _____

12PM–1PM _____   9PM–10PM _____

1PM–2PM _____   10PM–11PM _____

☐ Did I include enough breaks in the day?   ☐ Did I schedule my #1 most important thing?

EVENING REVIEW

Today was awesome because _____

_____

Today I struggled with _____

_____

On a scale of 1–10, with 10 being the highest, I would rate today's productivity at a...   1 2 3 4 5 6 7 8 9 10

Tomorrow I will...   Other Thoughts/Notes

DAILY ACTION PLAN

Date: _____ / _____ / _____   S M T W Th F S

"You can't cross the sea merely by standing and staring at the water."
—RABINDRANATH TAGORE

MORNING ROUTINE

Wake-up time _____   Water ☐   Exercise ☐   Daily Journal ☐   _____ ☐

This morning, I'm grateful for _____

GOALS AND M.I.N.S.

Goals are important to review daily, reinforcing your objectives to your conscious and subconscious mind. But goals alone are not enough. It's also vital that you take time to identify your Most Important Next Step (M.I.N.S.) for each goal, so your goal transforms into an action. And remember, when it comes to M.I.N.S., be specific.

Real Estate Goal: _____

Weekly Objective: _____

M.I.N.S. _____

Second Goal: _____

Weekly Objective: _____

M.I.N.S. _____

Third Goal: _____

Weekly Objective: _____

M.I.N.S. _____

I can consider today a "win" if I _____

Now, go place this on your time-blocking calendar for today.

REAL ESTATE L.A.P.S. FUNNEL

Use this space to set a daily goal for defining how you'll get **leads**, how many properties you'll **analyze**, how many properties you'll **pursue** (offer), and how many you'll **purchase** today.

GOAL   REALITY

LEADS

ANALYZE

PURSUE

$

TODAY'S TIME-BLOCKING ACTIVITIES

High-achieving real estate investors know that what gets scheduled gets done.
Take a few minutes to think about your goals, your M.I.N.S., and schedule your day.
Don't forget to include several breaks.

5AM–6AM _____   2PM–3PM _____

6AM–7AM _____   3PM–4PM _____

7AM–8AM _____   4PM–5PM _____

8AM–9AM _____   5PM–6PM _____

9AM–10AM _____   6PM–7PM _____

10AM–11AM _____   7PM–8PM _____

11AM–12PM _____   8PM–9PM _____

12PM–1PM _____   9PM–10PM _____

1PM–2PM _____   10PM–11PM _____

☐ Did I include enough breaks in the day?   ☐ Did I schedule my #1 most important thing?

EVENING REVIEW

Today was awesome because _____

_____

Today I struggled with _____

_____

On a scale of 1–10, with 10 being the highest, I would rate today's
productivity at a...   1 2 3 4 5 6 7 8 9 10

Tomorrow I will...   Other Thoughts/Notes

_____   _____

_____   _____

_____   _____

_____   _____

_____   _____

_____   _____

DAILY ACTION PLAN

Date: ____ / ____ / ____   S M T W Th F S

MORNING ROUTINE

Wake-up time _____   Water ☐   Exercise ☐   Daily Journal ☐   _____ ☐

This morning, I'm grateful for _____

GOALS AND M.I.N.S.

Goals are important to review daily, reinforcing your objectives to your conscious and subconscious mind. But goals alone are not enough. It's also vital that you take time to identify your Most Important Next Step (M.I.N.S.) for each goal, so your goal transforms into an action. And remember, when it comes to M.I.N.S., be specific.

Real Estate Goal: _____

Weekly Objective: _____

M.I.N.S. _____

Second Goal: _____

Weekly Objective: _____

M.I.N.S. _____

Third Goal: _____

Weekly Objective: _____

M.I.N.S. _____

I can consider today a "win" if I _____

Now, go place this on your time-blocking calendar for today.

REAL ESTATE L.A.P.S. FUNNEL

Use this space to set a daily goal for defining how you'll get **leads**, how many properties you'll **analyze**, how many properties you'll **pursue** (offer), and how many you'll **purchase** today.

GOAL   REALITY

LEADS

ANALYZE

PURSUE

$

TODAY'S TIME-BLOCKING ACTIVITIES

High-achieving real estate investors know that what gets scheduled gets done.
Take a few minutes to think about your goals, your M.I.N.S., and schedule your day.
Don't forget to include several breaks.

5AM–6AM _____

6AM–7AM _____

7AM–8AM _____

8AM–9AM _____

9AM–10AM _____

10AM–11AM _____

11AM–12PM _____

12PM–1PM _____

1PM–2PM _____

2PM–3PM _____

3PM–4PM _____

4PM–5PM _____

5PM–6PM _____

6PM–7PM _____

7PM–8PM _____

8PM–9PM _____

9PM–10PM _____

10PM–11PM _____

☐ Did I include enough breaks in the day?

☐ Did I schedule my #1 most important thing?

EVENING REVIEW

Today was awesome because _____

_____

Today I struggled with _____

_____

On a scale of 1–10, with 10 being the highest, I would rate today's
productivity at a...   1 2 3 4 5 6 7 8 9 10

Tomorrow I will...

Other Thoughts/Notes

DAILY ACTION PLAN

Date: ____ /____ /____

"Do the difficult things while they are easy and do the great things while they are small. A journey of a thousand miles must begin with a single step."

—Lao Tzu

MORNING ROUTINE

Wake-up time _____   Water ☐   Exercise ☐   Daily Journal ☐   _____ ☐

This morning, I'm grateful for _____

GOALS AND M.I.N.S.

Goals are important to review daily, reinforcing your objectives to your conscious and subconscious mind. But goals alone are not enough. It's also vital that you take time to identify your Most Important Next Step (M.I.N.S.) for each goal, so your goal transforms into an action. And remember, when it comes to M.I.N.S., be specific.

Real Estate Goal: _____

Weekly Objective: _____

M.I.N.S. _____

Second Goal: _____

Weekly Objective: _____

M.I.N.S. _____

Third Goal: _____

Weekly Objective: _____

M.I.N.S. _____

I can consider today a "win" if I _____

Now, go place this on your time-blocking calendar for today.

REAL ESTATE L.A.P.S. FUNNEL

Use this space to set a daily goal for defining how you'll get **leads**, how many properties you'll **analyze**, how many properties you'll **pursue** (offer), and how many you'll **purchase** today.

GOAL   REALITY

LEADS

ANALYZE

PURSUE

$

TODAY'S TIME-BLOCKING ACTIVITIES

High-achieving real estate investors know that what gets scheduled gets done.
Take a few minutes to think about your goals, your M.I.N.S., and schedule your day.
Don't forget to include several breaks.

5AM–6AM _____	2PM–3PM _____
6AM–7AM _____	3PM–4PM _____
7AM–8AM _____	4PM–5PM _____
8AM–9AM _____	5PM–6PM _____
9AM–10AM _____	6PM–7PM _____
10AM–11AM _____	7PM–8PM _____
11AM–12PM _____	8PM–9PM _____
12PM–1PM _____	9PM–10PM _____
1PM–2PM _____	10PM–11PM _____

☐ Did I include enough breaks in the day?

☐ Did I schedule my #1 most important thing?

EVENING REVIEW

Today was awesome because _____

_____

Today I struggled with _____

_____

On a scale of 1–10, with 10 being the highest, I would rate today's
productivity at a...   1 2 3 4 5 6 7 8 9 10

Tomorrow I will...   Other Thoughts/Notes

_____   _____

_____   _____

_____   _____

_____   _____

_____   _____

_____   _____

DAILY ACTION PLAN

Date: _____ / _____ / _____

S M T W Th F S

"Quality is not an act, it is a habit."
—ARISTOTLE

MORNING ROUTINE

Wake-up time _____ Water ☐ Exercise ☐ Daily Journal ☐ _____ ☐

This morning, I'm grateful for _____

GOALS AND M.I.N.S.

Goals are important to review daily, reinforcing your objectives to your conscious and subconscious mind. But goals alone are not enough. It's also vital that you take time to identify your Most Important Next Step (M.I.N.S.) for each goal, so your goal transforms into an action. And remember, when it comes to M.I.N.S., be specific.

Real Estate Goal: _____

Weekly Objective: _____

M.I.N.S. _____

Second Goal: _____

Weekly Objective: _____

M.I.N.S. _____

Third Goal: _____

Weekly Objective: _____

M.I.N.S. _____

I can consider today a "win" if I _____

Now, go place this on your time-blocking calendar for today.

REAL ESTATE L.A.P.S. FUNNEL

Use this space to set a daily goal for defining how you'll get **leads**, how many properties you'll **analyze**, how many properties you'll **pursue** (offer), and how many you'll **purchase** today.

GOAL

REALITY

LEADS

ANALYZE

PURSUE

$

TODAY'S TIME-BLOCKING ACTIVITIES

High-achieving real estate investors know that what gets scheduled gets done.
Take a few minutes to think about your goals, your M.I.N.S., and schedule your day.
Don't forget to include several breaks.

5AM–6AM _____   2PM–3PM _____

6AM–7AM _____   3PM–4PM _____

7AM–8AM _____   4PM–5PM _____

8AM–9AM _____   5PM–6PM _____

9AM–10AM _____   6PM–7PM _____

10AM–11AM _____   7PM–8PM _____

11AM–12PM _____   8PM–9PM _____

12PM–1PM _____   9PM–10PM _____

1PM–2PM _____   10PM–11PM _____

☐ Did I include enough breaks in the day?   ☐ Did I schedule my #1 most important thing?

EVENING REVIEW

Today was awesome because _____

_____

Today I struggled with _____

_____

On a scale of 1–10, with 10 being the highest, I would rate today's
productivity at a...   1 2 3 4 5 6 7 8 9 10

Tomorrow I will...   Other Thoughts/Notes

_____   _____

_____   _____

_____   _____

_____   _____

_____   _____

_____   _____

DAILY ACTION PLAN

Date: ____ / ____ / ____   S M T W Th F S

"If you can dream it, you can do it."
—WALT DISNEY

MORNING ROUTINE

Wake-up time _____ Water ☐ Exercise ☐ Daily Journal ☐ _____ ☐

This morning, I'm grateful for _____

GOALS AND M.I.N.S.

Goals are important to review daily, reinforcing your objectives to your conscious and subconscious mind. But goals alone are not enough. It's also vital that you take time to identify your Most Important Next Step (M.I.N.S.) for each goal, so your goal transforms into an action. And remember, when it comes to M.I.N.S., be specific.

Real Estate Goal: _____

Weekly Objective: _____

M.I.N.S. _____

Second Goal: _____

Weekly Objective: _____

M.I.N.S. _____

Third Goal: _____

Weekly Objective: _____

M.I.N.S. _____

I can consider today a "win" if I _____

Now, go place this on your time-blocking calendar for today.

REAL ESTATE L.A.P.S. FUNNEL

Use this space to set a daily goal for defining how you'll get **leads**, how many properties you'll **analyze**, how many properties you'll **pursue** (offer), and how many you'll **purchase** today.

GOAL   REALITY

LEADS

ANALYZE

PURSUE

$

TODAY'S TIME-BLOCKING ACTIVITIES

High-achieving real estate investors know that what gets scheduled gets done.
Take a few minutes to think about your goals, your M.I.N.S., and schedule your day.
Don't forget to include several breaks.

5AM–6AM _____	2PM–3PM _____
6AM–7AM _____	3PM–4PM _____
7AM–8AM _____	4PM–5PM _____
8AM–9AM _____	5PM–6PM _____
9AM–10AM _____	6PM–7PM _____
10AM–11AM _____	7PM–8PM _____
11AM–12PM _____	8PM–9PM _____
12PM–1PM _____	9PM–10PM _____
1PM–2PM _____	10PM–11PM _____

☐ Did I include enough breaks in the day?   ☐ Did I schedule my #1 most important thing?

EVENING REVIEW

Today was awesome because _____

_____

Today I struggled with _____

_____

On a scale of 1–10, with 10 being the highest, I would rate today's productivity at a...   1 2 3 4 5 6 7 8 9 10

Tomorrow I will...   Other Thoughts/Notes

DAILY ACTION PLAN

Date: ____ / ____ / ____   S M T W Th F S

"Your talent is God's gift to you.
What you do with it is your gift back to God."
—Leo Buscaglia

MORNING ROUTINE

Wake-up time _____   Water ☐   Exercise ☐   Daily Journal ☐   _____ ☐

This morning, I'm grateful for _____

GOALS AND M.I.N.S.

Goals are important to review daily, reinforcing your objectives to your conscious and subconscious mind. But goals alone are not enough. It's also vital that you take time to identify your Most Important Next Step (M.I.N.S.) for each goal, so your goal transforms into an action. And remember, when it comes to M.I.N.S., be specific.

Real Estate Goal: _____

Weekly Objective: _____

M.I.N.S. _____

Second Goal: _____

Weekly Objective: _____

M.I.N.S. _____

Third Goal: _____

Weekly Objective: _____

M.I.N.S. _____

I can consider today a "win" if I _____

Now, go place this on your time-blocking calendar for today.

REAL ESTATE L.A.P.S. FUNNEL

Use this space to set a daily goal for defining how you'll get **leads**, how many properties you'll **analyze**, how many properties you'll **pursue** (offer), and how many you'll **purchase** today.

GOAL   REALITY

LEADS

ANALYZE

PURSUE

$

TODAY'S TIME-BLOCKING ACTIVITIES

High-achieving real estate investors know that what gets scheduled gets done.
Take a few minutes to think about your goals, your M.I.N.S., and schedule your day.
Don't forget to include several breaks.

5AM–6AM _____	2PM–3PM _____
6AM–7AM _____	3PM–4PM _____
7AM–8AM _____	4PM–5PM _____
8AM–9AM _____	5PM–6PM _____
9AM–10AM _____	6PM–7PM _____
10AM–11AM _____	7PM–8PM _____
11AM–12PM _____	8PM–9PM _____
12PM–1PM _____	9PM–10PM _____
1PM–2PM _____	10PM–11PM _____

☐ Did I include enough breaks in the day?

☐ Did I schedule my #1 most important thing?

EVENING REVIEW

Today was awesome because _____

_____

Today I struggled with _____

_____

On a scale of 1–10, with 10 being the highest, I would rate today's productivity at a...   1 2 3 4 5 6 7 8 9 10

Tomorrow I will...

Other Thoughts/Notes

Date: _____ / _____ / _____ # DAILY ACTION PLAN S M T W Th F S

"The secret to getting ahead is getting started."
—Mark Twain

MORNING ROUTINE

Wake-up time _____ Water ☐ Exercise ☐ Daily Journal ☐ _____ ☐

This morning, I'm grateful for _____

GOALS AND M.I.N.S.

Goals are important to review daily, reinforcing your objectives to your conscious and subconscious mind. But goals alone are not enough. It's also vital that you take time to identify your Most Important Next Step (M.I.N.S.) for each goal, so your goal transforms into an action. And remember, when it comes to M.I.N.S., be specific.

Real Estate Goal: _____

Weekly Objective: _____

M.I.N.S. _____

Second Goal: _____

Weekly Objective: _____

M.I.N.S. _____

Third Goal: _____

Weekly Objective: _____

M.I.N.S. _____

I can consider today a "win" if I _____

Now, go place this on your time-blocking calendar for today.

REAL ESTATE L.A.P.S. FUNNEL

Use this space to set a daily goal for defining how you'll get **leads**, how many properties you'll **analyze**, how many properties you'll **pursue** (offer), and how many you'll **purchase** today.

GOAL   REALITY

LEADS

ANALYZE

PURSUE

$

TODAY'S TIME-BLOCKING ACTIVITIES

High-achieving real estate investors know that what gets scheduled gets done.
Take a few minutes to think about your goals, your M.I.N.S., and schedule your day.
Don't forget to include several breaks.

5AM–6AM _____	2PM–3PM _____
6AM–7AM _____	3PM–4PM _____
7AM–8AM _____	4PM–5PM _____
8AM–9AM _____	5PM–6PM _____
9AM–10AM _____	6PM–7PM _____
10AM–11AM _____	7PM–8PM _____
11AM–12PM _____	8PM–9PM _____
12PM–1PM _____	9PM–10PM _____
1PM–2PM _____	10PM–11PM _____

☐ Did I include enough breaks in the day?

☐ Did I schedule my #1 most important thing?

EVENING REVIEW

Today was awesome because _____

_____

Today I struggled with _____

_____

On a scale of 1–10, with 10 being the highest, I would rate today's
productivity at a...   1 2 3 4 5 6 7 8 9 10

Tomorrow I will...

Other Thoughts/Notes

Date: ___ / ___ / ___   # DAILY ACTION PLAN   S M T W Th F S

"If you want to conquer fear, don't sit home and think about it.
Go out and get busy."
—DALE CARNEGIE

MORNING ROUTINE

Wake-up time _____   Water ☐   Exercise ☐   Daily Journal ☐   _____ ☐

This morning, I'm grateful for _____

GOALS AND M.I.N.S.

Goals are important to review daily, reinforcing your objectives to your conscious and
subconscious mind. But goals alone are not enough. It's also vital that you take time to
identify your Most Important Next Step (M.I.N.S.) for each goal, so your goal transforms
into an action. And remember, when it comes to M.I.N.S., be specific.

Real Estate Goal: _____

Weekly Objective: _____

M.I.N.S. _____

Second Goal: _____

Weekly Objective: _____

M.I.N.S. _____

Third Goal: _____

Weekly Objective: _____

M.I.N.S. _____

I can consider today a "win" if I _____

Now, go place this on your time-blocking calendar for today.

REAL ESTATE L.A.P.S. FUNNEL

Use this space to set a daily goal for
defining how you'll get **leads**, how many
properties you'll **analyze**, how many
properties you'll **pursue** (offer), and how
many you'll **purchase** today.

GOAL   REALITY

LEADS
_____
ANALYZE
_____
PURSUE
_____
$
_____

TODAY'S TIME-BLOCKING ACTIVITIES

High-achieving real estate investors know that what gets scheduled gets done.
Take a few minutes to think about your goals, your M.I.N.S., and schedule your day.
Don't forget to include several breaks.

5AM–6AM _____	2PM–3PM _____
6AM–7AM _____	3PM–4PM _____
7AM–8AM _____	4PM–5PM _____
8AM–9AM _____	5PM–6PM _____
9AM–10AM _____	6PM–7PM _____
10AM–11AM _____	7PM–8PM _____
11AM–12PM _____	8PM–9PM _____
12PM–1PM _____	9PM–10PM _____
1PM–2PM _____	10PM–11PM _____

☐ Did I include enough breaks in the day?

☐ Did I schedule my #1 most important thing?

EVENING REVIEW

Today was awesome because _____

_____

Today I struggled with _____

_____

On a scale of 1–10, with 10 being the highest, I would rate today's
productivity at a...   1   2   3   4   5   6   7   8   9   10

Tomorrow I will...   Other Thoughts/Notes

Date: ____ / ____ / ____   # DAILY ACTION PLAN   S M T W Th F S

"We should not give up and we should not allow the problem to defeat us."
—A.P. J. Abdul Kalam

MORNING ROUTINE

Wake-up time _____ Water ☐ Exercise ☐ Daily Journal ☐ _____ ☐

This morning, I'm grateful for _____

GOALS AND M.I.N.S.

Goals are important to review daily, reinforcing your objectives to your conscious and subconscious mind. But goals alone are not enough. It's also vital that you take time to identify your Most Important Next Step (M.I.N.S.) for each goal, so your goal transforms into an action. And remember, when it comes to M.I.N.S., be specific.

Real Estate Goal: _____

Weekly Objective: _____

M.I.N.S. _____

Second Goal: _____

Weekly Objective: _____

M.I.N.S. _____

Third Goal: _____

Weekly Objective: _____

M.I.N.S. _____

I can consider today a "win" if I _____

Now, go place this on your time-blocking calendar for today.

REAL ESTATE L.A.P.S. FUNNEL

Use this space to set a daily goal for defining how you'll get **leads**, how many properties you'll **analyze**, how many properties you'll **pursue** (offer), and how many you'll **purchase** today.

GOAL   REALITY

LEADS

ANALYZE

PURSUE

$

TODAY'S TIME-BLOCKING ACTIVITIES

High-achieving real estate investors know that what gets scheduled gets done.
Take a few minutes to think about your goals, your M.I.N.S., and schedule your day.
Don't forget to include several breaks.

5AM–6AM _____	2PM–3PM _____
6AM–7AM _____	3PM–4PM _____
7AM–8AM _____	4PM–5PM _____
8AM–9AM _____	5PM–6PM _____
9AM–10AM _____	6PM–7PM _____
10AM–11AM _____	7PM–8PM _____
11AM–12PM _____	8PM–9PM _____
12PM–1PM _____	9PM–10PM _____
1PM–2PM _____	10PM–11PM _____

☐ Did I include enough breaks in the day?　　　☐ Did I schedule my #1 most important thing?

EVENING REVIEW

Today was awesome because _____

_____

Today I struggled with _____

_____

On a scale of 1–10, with 10 being the highest, I would rate today's
productivity at a...　　1　2　3　4　5　6　7　8　9　10

Tomorrow I will...　　　　　　　　　　Other Thoughts/Notes

_____　　　　_____

_____　　　　_____

_____　　　　_____

_____　　　　_____

_____　　　　_____

_____　　　　_____

Date: ____ / ____ / ____ # DAILY ACTION PLAN S M T W Th F S

"The best leaders have a high consideration factor.
They really care about their people."
—Brian Tracy

MORNING ROUTINE

Wake-up time _____ Water ☐ Exercise ☐ Daily Journal ☐ _____ ☐

This morning, I'm grateful for _____

GOALS AND M.I.N.S.

Goals are important to review daily, reinforcing your objectives to your conscious and subconscious mind. But goals alone are not enough. It's also vital that you take time to identify your Most Important Next Step (M.I.N.S.) for each goal, so your goal transforms into an action. And remember, when it comes to M.I.N.S., be specific.

Real Estate Goal: _____

Weekly Objective: _____

M.I.N.S. _____

Second Goal: _____

Weekly Objective: _____

M.I.N.S. _____

Third Goal: _____

Weekly Objective: _____

M.I.N.S. _____

I can consider today a "win" if I _____

Now, go place this on your time-blocking calendar for today.

REAL ESTATE L.A.P.S. FUNNEL

Use this space to set a daily goal for defining how you'll get **leads**, how many properties you'll **analyze**, how many properties you'll **pursue** (offer), and how many you'll **purchase** today.

GOAL   REALITY

LEADS

ANALYZE

PURSUE

$

TODAY'S TIME-BLOCKING ACTIVITIES

High-achieving real estate investors know that what gets scheduled gets done.
Take a few minutes to think about your goals, your M.I.N.S., and schedule your day.
Don't forget to include several breaks.

5AM–6AM _____	2PM–3PM _____
6AM–7AM _____	3PM–4PM _____
7AM–8AM _____	4PM–5PM _____
8AM–9AM _____	5PM–6PM _____
9AM–10AM _____	6PM–7PM _____
10AM–11AM _____	7PM–8PM _____
11AM–12PM _____	8PM–9PM _____
12PM–1PM _____	9PM–10PM _____
1PM–2PM _____	10PM–11PM _____

☐ Did I include enough breaks in the day?

☐ Did I schedule my #1 most important thing?

EVENING REVIEW

Today was awesome because _____

_____

Today I struggled with _____

_____

On a scale of 1–10, with 10 being the highest, I would rate today's
productivity at a...   1   2   3   4   5   6   7   8   9   10

Tomorrow I will...

Other Thoughts/Notes

DAILY ACTION PLAN

Date: ___ / ___ / ___   S M T W Th F S

*"There's only one corner of the universe you can be certain
of improving, and that's your own self."*
—ALDOUS HUXLEY

MORNING ROUTINE

Wake-up time _____ Water ☐ Exercise ☐ Daily Journal ☐ _____ ☐

This morning, I'm grateful for _____

GOALS AND M.I.N.S.

*Goals are important to review daily, reinforcing your objectives to your conscious and
subconscious mind. But goals alone are not enough. It's also vital that you take time to
identify your Most Important Next Step (M.I.N.S.) for each goal, so your goal transforms
into an action. And remember, when it comes to M.I.N.S., be specific.*

Real Estate Goal: _____

Weekly Objective: _____

M.I.N.S. _____

Second Goal: _____

Weekly Objective: _____

M.I.N.S. _____

Third Goal: _____

Weekly Objective: _____

M.I.N.S. _____

I can consider today a "win" if I _____

Now, go place this on your time-blocking calendar for today.

REAL ESTATE L.A.P.S. FUNNEL

Use this space to set a daily goal for
defining how you'll get **leads**, how many
properties you'll **analyze**, how many
properties you'll **pursue** (offer), and how
many you'll **purchase** today.

GOAL   REALITY

LEADS

ANALYZE

PURSUE

$

TODAY'S TIME-BLOCKING ACTIVITIES

High-achieving real estate investors know that what gets scheduled gets done.
Take a few minutes to think about your goals, your M.I.N.S., and schedule your day.
Don't forget to include several breaks.

5AM–6AM _____   2PM–3PM _____

6AM–7AM _____   3PM–4PM _____

7AM–8AM _____   4PM–5PM _____

8AM–9AM _____   5PM–6PM _____

9AM–10AM _____   6PM–7PM _____

10AM–11AM _____   7PM–8PM _____

11AM–12PM _____   8PM–9PM _____

12PM–1PM _____   9PM–10PM _____

1PM–2PM _____   10PM–11PM _____

☐ Did I include enough breaks
in the day?

☐ Did I schedule my #1 most
important thing?

EVENING REVIEW

Today was awesome because _____

_____

Today I struggled with _____

_____

On a scale of 1–10, with 10 being the highest, I would rate today's
productivity at a...   1 2 3 4 5 6 7 8 9 10

Tomorrow I will...   Other Thoughts/Notes

_____   _____

_____   _____

_____   _____

_____   _____

_____   _____

_____   _____

DAILY ACTION PLAN

"Accept the challenges so that you can feel the exhilaration of victory."
—GEORGE S. PATTON

MORNING ROUTINE

Wake-up time _____   Water ☐ Exercise ☐ Daily Journal ☐ _____ ☐

This morning, I'm grateful for _____

GOALS AND M.I.N.S.

Goals are important to review daily, reinforcing your objectives to your conscious and subconscious mind. But goals alone are not enough. It's also vital that you take time to identify your Most Important Next Step (M.I.N.S.) for each goal, so your goal transforms into an action. And remember, when it comes to M.I.N.S., be specific.

Real Estate Goal: _____

Weekly Objective: _____

M.I.N.S. _____

Second Goal: _____

Weekly Objective: _____

M.I.N.S. _____

Third Goal: _____

Weekly Objective: _____

M.I.N.S. _____

I can consider today a "win" if I _____

Now, go place this on your time-blocking calendar for today.

REAL ESTATE L.A.P.S. FUNNEL

Use this space to set a daily goal for defining how you'll get **leads**, how many properties you'll **analyze**, how many properties you'll **pursue** (offer), and how many you'll **purchase** today.

GOAL   REALITY

LEADS

ANALYZE

PURSUE

$

TODAY'S TIME-BLOCKING ACTIVITIES

High-achieving real estate investors know that what gets scheduled gets done.
Take a few minutes to think about your goals, your M.I.N.S., and schedule your day.
Don't forget to include several breaks.

5AM–6AM	_____	2PM–3PM	_____
6AM–7AM	_____	3PM–4PM	_____
7AM–8AM	_____	4PM–5PM	_____
8AM–9AM	_____	5PM–6PM	_____
9AM–10AM	_____	6PM–7PM	_____
10AM–11AM	_____	7PM–8PM	_____
11AM–12PM	_____	8PM–9PM	_____
12PM–1PM	_____	9PM–10PM	_____
1PM–2PM	_____	10PM–11PM	_____

☐ Did I include enough breaks in the day?

☐ Did I schedule my #1 most important thing?

EVENING REVIEW

Today was awesome because _____

_____

Today I struggled with _____

_____

On a scale of 1–10, with 10 being the highest, I would rate today's
productivity at a...   1 2 3 4 5 6 7 8 9 10

Tomorrow I will...   Other Thoughts/Notes

DAILY ACTION PLAN

Date: ___ / ___ / ___   S M T W Th F S

MORNING ROUTINE

Wake-up time _____   Water ☐   Exercise ☐   Daily Journal ☐   _____ ☐

This morning, I'm grateful for _____

GOALS AND M.I.N.S.

Goals are important to review daily, reinforcing your objectives to your conscious and subconscious mind. But goals alone are not enough. It's also vital that you take time to identify your Most Important Next Step (M.I.N.S.) for each goal, so your goal transforms into an action. And remember, when it comes to M.I.N.S., be specific.

Real Estate Goal: _____

Weekly Objective: _____

M.I.N.S. _____

Second Goal: _____

Weekly Objective: _____

M.I.N.S. _____

Third Goal: _____

Weekly Objective: _____

M.I.N.S. _____

I can consider today a "win" if I _____

Now, go place this on your time-blocking calendar for today.

REAL ESTATE L.A.P.S. FUNNEL

Use this space to set a daily goal for defining how you'll get **leads**, how many properties you'll **analyze**, how many properties you'll **pursue** (offer), and how many you'll **purchase** today.

GOAL   REALITY

LEADS

ANALYZE

PURSUE

$

TODAY'S TIME-BLOCKING ACTIVITIES

High-achieving real estate investors know that what gets scheduled gets done.
Take a few minutes to think about your goals, your M.I.N.S., and schedule your day.
Don't forget to include several breaks.

5AM–6AM _____	2PM–3PM _____
6AM–7AM _____	3PM–4PM _____
7AM–8AM _____	4PM–5PM _____
8AM–9AM _____	5PM–6PM _____
9AM–10AM _____	6PM–7PM _____
10AM–11AM _____	7PM–8PM _____
11AM–12PM _____	8PM–9PM _____
12PM–1PM _____	9PM–10PM _____
1PM–2PM _____	10PM–11PM _____

☐ Did I include enough breaks in the day?

☐ Did I schedule my #1 most important thing?

EVENING REVIEW

Today was awesome because _____

_____

Today I struggled with _____

_____

On a scale of 1–10, with 10 being the highest, I would rate today's
productivity at a...   1 2 3 4 5 6 7 8 9 10

Tomorrow I will...   Other Thoughts/Notes

Date: ___ / ___ / ___   # DAILY ACTION PLAN

"When something is important enough,
you do it even if the odds are not in your favor."
—ELON MUSK

MORNING ROUTINE

Wake-up time _____ Water ☐ Exercise ☐ Daily Journal ☐ _____ ☐

This morning, I'm grateful for _____

GOALS AND M.I.N.S.

Goals are important to review daily, reinforcing your objectives to your conscious and subconscious mind. But goals alone are not enough. It's also vital that you take time to identify your Most Important Next Step (M.I.N.S.) for each goal, so your goal transforms into an action. And remember, when it comes to M.I.N.S., be specific.

Real Estate Goal: _____

Weekly Objective: _____

M.I.N.S. _____

Second Goal: _____

Weekly Objective: _____

M.I.N.S. _____

Third Goal: _____

Weekly Objective: _____

M.I.N.S. _____

I can consider today a "win" if I _____

Now, go place this on your time-blocking calendar for today.

REAL ESTATE L.A.P.S. FUNNEL

Use this space to set a daily goal for defining how you'll get **leads**, how many properties you'll **analyze**, how many properties you'll **pursue** (offer), and how many you'll **purchase** today.

GOAL   REALITY

LEADS

ANALYZE

PURSUE

$

TODAY'S TIME-BLOCKING ACTIVITIES

High-achieving real estate investors know that what gets scheduled gets done.
Take a few minutes to think about your goals, your M.I.N.S., and schedule your day.
Don't forget to include several breaks.

5AM–6AM _____   2PM–3PM _____

6AM–7AM _____   3PM–4PM _____

7AM–8AM _____   4PM–5PM _____

8AM–9AM _____   5PM–6PM _____

9AM–10AM _____   6PM–7PM _____

10AM–11AM _____   7PM–8PM _____

11AM–12PM _____   8PM–9PM _____

12PM–1PM _____   9PM–10PM _____

1PM–2PM _____   10PM–11PM _____

☐ Did I include enough breaks in the day?   ☐ Did I schedule my #1 most important thing?

EVENING REVIEW

Today was awesome because _____

_____

Today I struggled with _____

_____

On a scale of 1–10, with 10 being the highest, I would rate today's
productivity at a...   1 2 3 4 5 6 7 8 9 10

Tomorrow I will...   Other Thoughts/Notes

Date: ____ / ____ / ____ # DAILY ACTION PLAN

"A somebody was once a nobody who wanted to and did."
—JOHN BURROUGHS

MORNING ROUTINE

Wake-up time _____ Water ☐ Exercise ☐ Daily Journal ☐ _____ ☐

This morning, I'm grateful for _____

GOALS AND M.I.N.S.

Goals are important to review daily, reinforcing your objectives to your conscious and subconscious mind. But goals alone are not enough. It's also vital that you take time to identify your Most Important Next Step (M.I.N.S.) for each goal, so your goal transforms into an action. And remember, when it comes to M.I.N.S., be specific.

Real Estate Goal: _____

Weekly Objective: _____

M.I.N.S. _____

Second Goal: _____

Weekly Objective: _____

M.I.N.S. _____

Third Goal: _____

Weekly Objective: _____

M.I.N.S. _____

I can consider today a "win" if I _____

Now, go place this on your time-blocking calendar for today.

REAL ESTATE L.A.P.S. FUNNEL

Use this space to set a daily goal for defining how you'll get **leads**, how many properties you'll **analyze**, how many properties you'll **pursue** (offer), and how many you'll **purchase** today.

GOAL   REALITY

LEADS

ANALYZE

PURSUE

$

TODAY'S TIME-BLOCKING ACTIVITIES

High-achieving real estate investors know that what gets scheduled gets done.
Take a few minutes to think about your goals, your M.I.N.S., and schedule your day.
Don't forget to include several breaks.

5AM–6AM _____	2PM–3PM _____
6AM–7AM _____	3PM–4PM _____
7AM–8AM _____	4PM–5PM _____
8AM–9AM _____	5PM–6PM _____
9AM–10AM _____	6PM–7PM _____
10AM–11AM _____	7PM–8PM _____
11AM–12PM _____	8PM–9PM _____
12PM–1PM _____	9PM–10PM _____
1PM–2PM _____	10PM–11PM _____

☐ Did I include enough breaks in the day?

☐ Did I schedule my #1 most important thing?

EVENING REVIEW

Today was awesome because _____

_____

Today I struggled with _____

_____

On a scale of 1–10, with 10 being the highest, I would rate today's
productivity at a...   1   2   3   4   5   6   7   8   9   10

Tomorrow I will...   Other Thoughts/Notes

_____   _____

_____   _____

_____   _____

_____   _____

_____   _____

_____   _____

DAILY ACTION PLAN

Date: ____ / ____ / ____

"A creative man is motivated by the desire to achieve,
not by the desire to beat others."

—AYN RAND

MORNING ROUTINE

Wake-up time _____ Water ☐ Exercise ☐ Daily Journal ☐ _____ ☐

This morning, I'm grateful for _____

GOALS AND M.I.N.S.

Goals are important to review daily, reinforcing your objectives to your conscious and subconscious mind. But goals alone are not enough. It's also vital that you take time to identify your Most Important Next Step (M.I.N.S.) for each goal, so your goal transforms into an action. And remember, when it comes to M.I.N.S., be specific.

Real Estate Goal: _____

Weekly Objective: _____

M.I.N.S. _____

Second Goal: _____

Weekly Objective: _____

M.I.N.S. _____

Third Goal: _____

Weekly Objective: _____

M.I.N.S. _____

I can consider today a "win" if I _____

Now, go place this on your time-blocking calendar for today.

REAL ESTATE L.A.P.S. FUNNEL

Use this space to set a daily goal for defining how you'll get **leads**, how many properties you'll **analyze**, how many properties you'll **pursue** (offer), and how many you'll **purchase** today.

GOAL   REALITY

LEADS

ANALYZE

PURSUE

$

TODAY'S TIME-BLOCKING ACTIVITIES

High-achieving real estate investors know that what gets scheduled gets done.
Take a few minutes to think about your goals, your M.I.N.S., and schedule your day.
Don't forget to include several breaks.

5AM–6AM _____	2PM–3PM _____
6AM–7AM _____	3PM–4PM _____
7AM–8AM _____	4PM–5PM _____
8AM–9AM _____	5PM–6PM _____
9AM–10AM _____	6PM–7PM _____
10AM–11AM _____	7PM–8PM _____
11AM–12PM _____	8PM–9PM _____
12PM–1PM _____	9PM–10PM _____
1PM–2PM _____	10PM–11PM _____

☐ Did I include enough breaks in the day?

☐ Did I schedule my #1 most important thing?

EVENING REVIEW

Today was awesome because _____

_____

Today I struggled with _____

_____

On a scale of 1–10, with 10 being the highest, I would rate today's
productivity at a...   1   2   3   4   5   6   7   8   9   10

Tomorrow I will...   Other Thoughts/Notes

DAILY ACTION PLAN

Date: ____ / ____ / ____   S M T W Th F S

"Set your goals high and don't stop until you get there."
—Bo Jackson

MORNING ROUTINE

Wake-up time _____   Water ☐ Exercise ☐ Daily Journal ☐   _____ ☐

This morning, I'm grateful for _____

GOALS AND M.I.N.S.

Goals are important to review daily, reinforcing your objectives to your conscious and subconscious mind. But goals alone are not enough. It's also vital that you take time to identify your Most Important Next Step (M.I.N.S.) for each goal, so your goal transforms into an action. And remember, when it comes to M.I.N.S., be specific.

Real Estate Goal: _____

Weekly Objective: _____

M.I.N.S. _____

Second Goal: _____

Weekly Objective: _____

M.I.N.S. _____

Third Goal: _____

Weekly Objective: _____

M.I.N.S. _____

I can consider today a "win" if I _____

Now, go place this on your time-blocking calendar for today.

REAL ESTATE L.A.P.S. FUNNEL

Use this space to set a daily goal for defining how you'll get **leads**, how many properties you'll **analyze**, how many properties you'll **pursue** (offer), and how many you'll **purchase** today.

GOAL   REALITY

LEADS

ANALYZE

PURSUE

$

TODAY'S TIME-BLOCKING ACTIVITIES

High-achieving real estate investors know that what gets scheduled gets done.
Take a few minutes to think about your goals, your M.I.N.S., and schedule your day.
Don't forget to include several breaks.

5AM–6AM _____

6AM–7AM _____

7AM–8AM _____

8AM–9AM _____

9AM–10AM _____

10AM–11AM _____

11AM–12PM _____

12PM–1PM _____

1PM–2PM _____

2PM–3PM _____

3PM–4PM _____

4PM–5PM _____

5PM–6PM _____

6PM–7PM _____

7PM–8PM _____

8PM–9PM _____

9PM–10PM _____

10PM–11PM _____

☐ Did I include enough breaks
in the day?

☐ Did I schedule my #1 most
important thing?

EVENING REVIEW

Today was awesome because _____

_____

Today I struggled with _____

_____

On a scale of 1–10, with 10 being the highest, I would rate today's
productivity at a...   1   2   3   4   5   6   7   8   9   10

Tomorrow I will...

Other Thoughts/Notes

Date: ____ / ____ / ____   # DAILY ACTION PLAN   S M T W Th F S

"Be kind whenever possible. It is always possible."
—DALAI LAMA

MORNING ROUTINE

Wake-up time _____   Water ☐ Exercise ☐ Daily Journal ☐ _____ ☐

This morning, I'm grateful for _____

GOALS AND M.I.N.S.

Goals are important to review daily, reinforcing your objectives to your conscious and subconscious mind. But goals alone are not enough. It's also vital that you take time to identify your Most Important Next Step (M.I.N.S.) for each goal, so your goal transforms into an action. And remember, when it comes to M.I.N.S., be specific.

Real Estate Goal: _____

Weekly Objective: _____

M.I.N.S. _____

Second Goal: _____

Weekly Objective: _____

M.I.N.S. _____

Third Goal: _____

Weekly Objective: _____

M.I.N.S. _____

I can consider today a "win" if I _____

Now, go place this on your time-blocking calendar for today.

REAL ESTATE L.A.P.S. FUNNEL

Use this space to set a daily goal for defining how you'll get **leads**, how many properties you'll **analyze**, how many properties you'll **pursue** (offer), and how many you'll **purchase** today.

GOAL   REALITY

LEADS

ANALYZE

PURSUE

$

TODAY'S TIME-BLOCKING ACTIVITIES

High-achieving real estate investors know that what gets scheduled gets done.
Take a few minutes to think about your goals, your M.I.N.S., and schedule your day.
Don't forget to include several breaks.

5AM–6AM _____   2PM–3PM _____

6AM–7AM _____   3PM–4PM _____

7AM–8AM _____   4PM–5PM _____

8AM–9AM _____   5PM–6PM _____

9AM–10AM _____   6PM–7PM _____

10AM–11AM _____   7PM–8PM _____

11AM–12PM _____   8PM–9PM _____

12PM–1PM _____   9PM–10PM _____

1PM–2PM _____   10PM–11PM _____

☐ Did I include enough breaks   ☐ Did I schedule my #1 most
   in the day?   important thing?

EVENING REVIEW

Today was awesome because _____

_____

Today I struggled with _____

_____

On a scale of 1–10, with 10 being the highest, I would rate today's
productivity at a...   1 2 3 4 5 6 7 8 9 10

Tomorrow I will...   Other Thoughts/Notes

_____   _____

_____   _____

_____   _____

_____   _____

_____   _____

_____   _____

DAILY ACTION PLAN

Date: ____ / ____ / ____   S M T W Th F S

MORNING ROUTINE

Wake-up time _____   Water ☐   Exercise ☐   Daily Journal ☐   _____ ☐

This morning, I'm grateful for _____

GOALS AND M.I.N.S.

Goals are important to review daily, reinforcing your objectives to your conscious and subconscious mind. But goals alone are not enough. It's also vital that you take time to identify your Most Important Next Step (M.I.N.S.) for each goal, so your goal transforms into an action. And remember, when it comes to M.I.N.S., be specific.

Real Estate Goal: _____

Weekly Objective: _____

M.I.N.S. _____

Second Goal: _____

Weekly Objective: _____

M.I.N.S. _____

Third Goal: _____

Weekly Objective: _____

M.I.N.S. _____

I can consider today a "win" if I _____

Now, go place this on your time-blocking calendar for today.

REAL ESTATE L.A.P.S. FUNNEL

Use this space to set a daily goal for defining how you'll get **leads**, how many properties you'll **analyze**, how many properties you'll **pursue** (offer), and how many you'll **purchase** today.

GOAL   REALITY

LEADS

ANALYZE

PURSUE

$

TODAY'S TIME-BLOCKING ACTIVITIES

High-achieving real estate investors know that what gets scheduled gets done.
Take a few minutes to think about your goals, your M.I.N.S., and schedule your day.
Don't forget to include several breaks.

5AM–6AM _____   2PM–3PM _____

6AM–7AM _____   3PM–4PM _____

7AM–8AM _____   4PM–5PM _____

8AM–9AM _____   5PM–6PM _____

9AM–10AM _____   6PM–7PM _____

10AM–11AM _____   7PM–8PM _____

11AM–12PM _____   8PM–9PM _____

12PM–1PM _____   9PM–10PM _____

1PM–2PM _____   10PM–11PM _____

☐ Did I include enough breaks in the day?   ☐ Did I schedule my #1 most important thing?

EVENING REVIEW

Today was awesome because _____

_____

Today I struggled with _____

_____

On a scale of 1–10, with 10 being the highest, I would rate today's
productivity at a...   1 2 3 4 5 6 7 8 9 10

Tomorrow I will...   Other Thoughts/Notes

_____   _____

_____   _____

_____   _____

_____   _____

_____   _____

_____   _____

Date: ____ / ____ / ____   # DAILY ACTION PLAN

"If you're going through hell, keep going."
—WINSTON CHURCHILL

MORNING ROUTINE

Wake-up time _____   Water ☐   Exercise ☐   Daily Journal ☐   _____ ☐

This morning, I'm grateful for _____

GOALS AND M.I.N.S.

Goals are important to review daily, reinforcing your objectives to your conscious and subconscious mind. But goals alone are not enough. It's also vital that you take time to identify your Most Important Next Step (M.I.N.S.) for each goal, so your goal transforms into an action. And remember, when it comes to M.I.N.S., be specific.

Real Estate Goal: _____

Weekly Objective: _____

M.I.N.S. _____

Second Goal: _____

Weekly Objective: _____

M.I.N.S. _____

Third Goal: _____

Weekly Objective: _____

M.I.N.S. _____

I can consider today a "win" if I _____

Now, go place this on your time-blocking calendar for today.

REAL ESTATE L.A.P.S. FUNNEL

Use this space to set a daily goal for defining how you'll get **leads**, how many properties you'll **analyze**, how many properties you'll **pursue** (offer), and how many you'll **purchase** today.

GOAL   REALITY

LEADS

ANALYZE

PURSUE

$

TODAY'S TIME-BLOCKING ACTIVITIES

High-achieving real estate investors know that what gets scheduled gets done.
Take a few minutes to think about your goals, your M.I.N.S., and schedule your day.
Don't forget to include several breaks.

5AM–6AM _____	2PM–3PM _____
6AM–7AM _____	3PM–4PM _____
7AM–8AM _____	4PM–5PM _____
8AM–9AM _____	5PM–6PM _____
9AM–10AM _____	6PM–7PM _____
10AM–11AM _____	7PM–8PM _____
11AM–12PM _____	8PM–9PM _____
12PM–1PM _____	9PM–10PM _____
1PM–2PM _____	10PM–11PM _____

☐ Did I include enough breaks in the day?

☐ Did I schedule my #1 most important thing?

EVENING REVIEW

Today was awesome because _____

_____

Today I struggled with _____

_____

On a scale of 1–10, with 10 being the highest, I would rate today's
productivity at a...   1   2   3   4   5   6   7   8   9   10

Tomorrow I will...   Other Thoughts/Notes

DAILY ACTION PLAN

"Problems are not stop signs, they are guidelines."
—Robert H. Schuller

MORNING ROUTINE

Wake-up time _____ Water ☐ Exercise ☐ Daily Journal ☐ _____ ☐

This morning, I'm grateful for _____

GOALS AND M.I.N.S.

Goals are important to review daily, reinforcing your objectives to your conscious and subconscious mind. But goals alone are not enough. It's also vital that you take time to identify your Most Important Next Step (M.I.N.S.) for each goal, so your goal transforms into an action. And remember, when it comes to M.I.N.S., be specific.

Real Estate Goal: _____

Weekly Objective: _____

M.I.N.S. _____

Second Goal: _____

Weekly Objective: _____

M.I.N.S. _____

Third Goal: _____

Weekly Objective: _____

M.I.N.S. _____

I can consider today a "win" if I _____

Now, go place this on your time-blocking calendar for today.

REAL ESTATE L.A.P.S. FUNNEL

Use this space to set a daily goal for defining how you'll get **leads**, how many properties you'll **analyze**, how many properties you'll **pursue** (offer), and how many you'll **purchase** today.

GOAL   REALITY

LEADS

ANALYZE

PURSUE

$

TODAY'S TIME-BLOCKING ACTIVITIES

High-achieving real estate investors know that what gets scheduled gets done.
Take a few minutes to think about your goals, your M.I.N.S., and schedule your day.
Don't forget to include several breaks.

5AM–6AM _____	2PM–3PM _____
6AM–7AM _____	3PM–4PM _____
7AM–8AM _____	4PM–5PM _____
8AM–9AM _____	5PM–6PM _____
9AM–10AM _____	6PM–7PM _____
10AM–11AM _____	7PM–8PM _____
11AM–12PM _____	8PM–9PM _____
12PM–1PM _____	9PM–10PM _____
1PM–2PM _____	10PM–11PM _____

☐ Did I include enough breaks in the day?

☐ Did I schedule my #1 most important thing?

EVENING REVIEW

Today was awesome because _____

_____

Today I struggled with _____

_____

On a scale of 1–10, with 10 being the highest, I would rate today's
productivity at a...   1 2 3 4 5 6 7 8 9 10

Tomorrow I will...   Other Thoughts/Notes

_____   _____

_____   _____

_____   _____

_____   _____

_____   _____

_____   _____

Date: ____ / ____ / ____   # DAILY ACTION PLAN

"Concern yourself not with what you tried and failed in,
but with what it is still possible for you to do."
—Pope John XXIII

MORNING ROUTINE

Wake-up time _____   Water ☐   Exercise ☐   Daily Journal ☐   _____ ☐

This morning, I'm grateful for _____

GOALS AND M.I.N.S.

Goals are important to review daily, reinforcing your objectives to your conscious and
subconscious mind. But goals alone are not enough. It's also vital that you take time to
identify your Most Important Next Step (M.I.N.S.) for each goal, so your goal transforms
into an action. And remember, when it comes to M.I.N.S., be specific.

Real Estate Goal: _____

Weekly Objective: _____

M.I.N.S. _____

Second Goal: _____

Weekly Objective: _____

M.I.N.S. _____

Third Goal: _____

Weekly Objective: _____

M.I.N.S. _____

I can consider today a "win" if I _____

Now, go place this on your time-blocking calendar for today.

REAL ESTATE L.A.P.S. FUNNEL

GOAL   REALITY

Use this space to set a daily goal for
defining how you'll get **leads**, how many
properties you'll **analyze**, how many
properties you'll **pursue** (offer), and how
many you'll **purchase** today.

LEADS

ANALYZE

PURSUE

$

TODAY'S TIME-BLOCKING ACTIVITIES

High-achieving real estate investors know that what gets scheduled gets done.
Take a few minutes to think about your goals, your M.I.N.S., and schedule your day.
Don't forget to include several breaks.

5AM–6AM _____	2PM–3PM _____
6AM–7AM _____	3PM–4PM _____
7AM–8AM _____	4PM–5PM _____
8AM–9AM _____	5PM–6PM _____
9AM–10AM _____	6PM–7PM _____
10AM–11AM _____	7PM–8PM _____
11AM–12PM _____	8PM–9PM _____
12PM–1PM _____	9PM–10PM _____
1PM–2PM _____	10PM–11PM _____

☐ Did I include enough breaks in the day?

☐ Did I schedule my #1 most important thing?

EVENING REVIEW

Today was awesome because _____

_____

Today I struggled with _____

_____

On a scale of 1–10, with 10 being the highest, I would rate today's
productivity at a...   1 2 3 4 5 6 7 8 9 10

Tomorrow I will...   Other Thoughts/Notes

DAILY ACTION PLAN

Date: ____ / ____ / ____

S M T W Th F S

MORNING ROUTINE

Wake-up time _____ Water ☐ Exercise ☐ Daily Journal ☐ _____ ☐

This morning, I'm grateful for _____

GOALS AND M.I.N.S.

Goals are important to review daily, reinforcing your objectives to your conscious and subconscious mind. But goals alone are not enough. It's also vital that you take time to identify your Most Important Next Step (M.I.N.S.) for each goal, so your goal transforms into an action. And remember, when it comes to M.I.N.S., be specific.

Real Estate Goal: _____

Weekly Objective: _____

M.I.N.S. _____

Second Goal: _____

Weekly Objective: _____

M.I.N.S. _____

Third Goal: _____

Weekly Objective: _____

M.I.N.S. _____

I can consider today a "win" if I _____

Now, go place this on your time-blocking calendar for today.

REAL ESTATE L.A.P.S. FUNNEL

Use this space to set a daily goal for defining how you'll get **leads**, how many properties you'll **analyze**, how many properties you'll **pursue** (offer), and how many you'll **purchase** today.

GOAL   REALITY

LEADS

ANALYZE

PURSUE

$

TODAY'S TIME-BLOCKING ACTIVITIES

High-achieving real estate investors know that what gets scheduled gets done.
Take a few minutes to think about your goals, your M.I.N.S., and schedule your day.
Don't forget to include several breaks.

5AM–6AM _____	2PM–3PM _____
6AM–7AM _____	3PM–4PM _____
7AM–8AM _____	4PM–5PM _____
8AM–9AM _____	5PM–6PM _____
9AM–10AM _____	6PM–7PM _____
10AM–11AM _____	7PM–8PM _____
11AM–12PM _____	8PM–9PM _____
12PM–1PM _____	9PM–10PM _____
1PM–2PM _____	10PM–11PM _____

☐ Did I include enough breaks in the day?

☐ Did I schedule my #1 most important thing?

EVENING REVIEW

Today was awesome because _____

_____

Today I struggled with _____

_____

On a scale of 1–10, with 10 being the highest, I would rate today's
productivity at a...   1   2   3   4   5   6   7   8   9   10

Tomorrow I will...   Other Thoughts/Notes

Date: ____ / ____ / ____　　# DAILY ACTION PLAN　　S M T W Th F S

MORNING ROUTINE

Wake-up time _____　Water ☐　Exercise ☐　Daily Journal ☐　_____ ☐

This morning, I'm grateful for _____

GOALS AND M.I.N.S.

Goals are important to review daily, reinforcing your objectives to your conscious and subconscious mind. But goals alone are not enough. It's also vital that you take time to identify your Most Important Next Step (M.I.N.S.) for each goal, so your goal transforms into an action. And remember, when it comes to M.I.N.S., be specific.

Real Estate Goal: _____

Weekly Objective: _____

M.I.N.S. _____

Second Goal: _____

Weekly Objective: _____

M.I.N.S. _____

Third Goal: _____

Weekly Objective: _____

M.I.N.S. _____

I can consider today a "win" if I _____

Now, go place this on your time-blocking calendar for today.

REAL ESTATE L.A.P.S. FUNNEL

Use this space to set a daily goal for defining how you'll get **leads**, how many properties you'll **analyze**, how many properties you'll **pursue** (offer), and how many you'll **purchase** today.

GOAL　　　　　　　　　　　REALITY

LEADS

ANALYZE

PURSUE

$

TODAY'S TIME-BLOCKING ACTIVITIES

High-achieving real estate investors know that what gets scheduled gets done.
Take a few minutes to think about your goals, your M.I.N.S., and schedule your day.
Don't forget to include several breaks.

5AM–6AM _____	2PM–3PM _____
6AM–7AM _____	3PM–4PM _____
7AM–8AM _____	4PM–5PM _____
8AM–9AM _____	5PM–6PM _____
9AM–10AM _____	6PM–7PM _____
10AM–11AM _____	7PM–8PM _____
11AM–12PM _____	8PM–9PM _____
12PM–1PM _____	9PM–10PM _____
1PM–2PM _____	10PM–11PM _____

☐ Did I include enough breaks in the day?

☐ Did I schedule my #1 most important thing?

EVENING REVIEW

Today was awesome because _____

_____

Today I struggled with _____

_____

On a scale of 1–10, with 10 being the highest, I would rate today's
productivity at a...   1 2 3 4 5 6 7 8 9 10

Tomorrow I will...   Other Thoughts/Notes

DAILY ACTION PLAN

"What you get by achieving your goals is not as important
as what you become by achieving your goals."
—Zig Ziglar

MORNING ROUTINE

Wake-up time _____   Water ☐   Exercise ☐   Daily Journal ☐   _____ ☐

This morning, I'm grateful for _____

GOALS AND M.I.N.S.

Goals are important to review daily, reinforcing your objectives to your conscious and
subconscious mind. But goals alone are not enough. It's also vital that you take time to
identify your Most Important Next Step (M.I.N.S.) for each goal, so your goal transforms
into an action. And remember, when it comes to M.I.N.S., be specific.

Real Estate Goal: _____

Weekly Objective: _____

M.I.N.S. _____

Second Goal: _____

Weekly Objective: _____

M.I.N.S. _____

Third Goal: _____

Weekly Objective: _____

M.I.N.S. _____

I can consider today a "win" if I _____

Now, go place this on your time-blocking calendar for today.

REAL ESTATE L.A.P.S. FUNNEL

Use this space to set a daily goal for
defining how you'll get **leads**, how many
properties you'll **analyze**, how many
properties you'll **pursue** (offer), and how
many you'll **purchase** today.

GOAL   REALITY

LEADS

ANALYZE

PURSUE

$

TODAY'S TIME-BLOCKING ACTIVITIES

High-achieving real estate investors know that what gets scheduled gets done.
Take a few minutes to think about your goals, your M.I.N.S., and schedule your day.
Don't forget to include several breaks.

5AM–6AM	_____	2PM–3PM	_____
6AM–7AM	_____	3PM–4PM	_____
7AM–8AM	_____	4PM–5PM	_____
8AM–9AM	_____	5PM–6PM	_____
9AM–10AM	_____	6PM–7PM	_____
10AM–11AM	_____	7PM–8PM	_____
11AM–12PM	_____	8PM–9PM	_____
12PM–1PM	_____	9PM–10PM	_____
1PM–2PM	_____	10PM–11PM	_____

☐ Did I include enough breaks in the day?

☐ Did I schedule my #1 most important thing?

EVENING REVIEW

Today was awesome because _____

_____

Today I struggled with _____

_____

On a scale of 1–10, with 10 being the highest, I would rate today's
productivity at a...   1   2   3   4   5   6   7   8   9   10

Tomorrow I will...

Other Thoughts/Notes

DAILY ACTION PLAN

Date: ____ / ____ / ____   S M T W Th F S

"Start where you are. Use what you have. Do what you can."
—ARTHUR ASHE

MORNING ROUTINE

Wake-up time _____   Water ☐   Exercise ☐   Daily Journal ☐   _____ ☐

This morning, I'm grateful for _____

GOALS AND M.I.N.S.

Goals are important to review daily, reinforcing your objectives to your conscious and subconscious mind. But goals alone are not enough. It's also vital that you take time to identify your Most Important Next Step (M.I.N.S.) for each goal, so your goal transforms into an action. And remember, when it comes to M.I.N.S., be specific.

Real Estate Goal: _____

Weekly Objective: _____

M.I.N.S. _____

Second Goal: _____

Weekly Objective: _____

M.I.N.S. _____

Third Goal: _____

Weekly Objective: _____

M.I.N.S. _____

I can consider today a "win" if I _____

Now, go place this on your time-blocking calendar for today.

REAL ESTATE L.A.P.S. FUNNEL

Use this space to set a daily goal for defining how you'll get **leads**, how many properties you'll **analyze**, how many properties you'll **pursue** (offer), and how many you'll **purchase** today.

GOAL   REALITY

LEADS

ANALYZE

PURSUE

$

TODAY'S TIME-BLOCKING ACTIVITIES

High-achieving real estate investors know that what gets scheduled gets done.
Take a few minutes to think about your goals, your M.I.N.S., and schedule your day.
Don't forget to include several breaks.

5AM–6AM _____	2PM–3PM _____
6AM–7AM _____	3PM–4PM _____
7AM–8AM _____	4PM–5PM _____
8AM–9AM _____	5PM–6PM _____
9AM–10AM _____	6PM–7PM _____
10AM–11AM _____	7PM–8PM _____
11AM–12PM _____	8PM–9PM _____
12PM–1PM _____	9PM–10PM _____
1PM–2PM _____	10PM–11PM _____

☐ Did I include enough breaks in the day?

☐ Did I schedule my #1 most important thing?

EVENING REVIEW

Today was awesome because _____

_____

Today I struggled with _____

_____

On a scale of 1–10, with 10 being the highest, I would rate today's
productivity at a...   1 2 3 4 5 6 7 8 9 10

Tomorrow I will...   Other Thoughts/Notes

_____   _____

_____   _____

_____   _____

_____   _____

_____   _____

_____   _____

DAILY ACTION PLAN

"Aim for the moon. If you miss, you may hit a star."
—W. CLEMENT STONE

MORNING ROUTINE

Wake-up time _____ Water ☐ Exercise ☐ Daily Journal ☐ _____ ☐

This morning, I'm grateful for _____

GOALS AND M.I.N.S.

Goals are important to review daily, reinforcing your objectives to your conscious and subconscious mind. But goals alone are not enough. It's also vital that you take time to identify your Most Important Next Step (M.I.N.S.) for each goal, so your goal transforms into an action. And remember, when it comes to M.I.N.S., be specific.

Real Estate Goal: _____

Weekly Objective: _____

M.I.N.S. _____

Second Goal: _____

Weekly Objective: _____

M.I.N.S. _____

Third Goal: _____

Weekly Objective: _____

M.I.N.S. _____

I can consider today a "win" if I _____

Now, go place this on your time-blocking calendar for today.

REAL ESTATE L.A.P.S. FUNNEL

Use this space to set a daily goal for defining how you'll get **leads**, how many properties you'll **analyze**, how many properties you'll **pursue** (offer), and how many you'll **purchase** today.

GOAL   REALITY

LEADS

ANALYZE

PURSUE

$

TODAY'S TIME-BLOCKING ACTIVITIES

High-achieving real estate investors know that what gets scheduled gets done.
Take a few minutes to think about your goals, your M.I.N.S., and schedule your day.
Don't forget to include several breaks.

5AM–6AM _____	2PM–3PM _____
6AM–7AM _____	3PM–4PM _____
7AM–8AM _____	4PM–5PM _____
8AM–9AM _____	5PM–6PM _____
9AM–10AM _____	6PM–7PM _____
10AM–11AM _____	7PM–8PM _____
11AM–12PM _____	8PM–9PM _____
12PM–1PM _____	9PM–10PM _____
1PM–2PM _____	10PM–11PM _____

☐ Did I include enough breaks in the day?

☐ Did I schedule my #1 most important thing?

EVENING REVIEW

Today was awesome because _____

_____

Today I struggled with _____

_____

On a scale of 1–10, with 10 being the highest, I would rate today's
productivity at a...   1   2   3   4   5   6   7   8   9   10

Tomorrow I will...   Other Thoughts/Notes

Date: ____ / ____ / ____ **DAILY ACTION PLAN** S M T W Th F S

"Remember to look up at the stars and not down at your feet. Try to make sense of what you see and wonder about what makes the universe exist."
—STEPHEN HAWKING

MORNING ROUTINE

Wake-up time _____ Water ☐ Exercise ☐ Daily Journal ☐ _____ ☐

This morning, I'm grateful for _____

GOALS AND M.I.N.S.

Goals are important to review daily, reinforcing your objectives to your conscious and subconscious mind. But goals alone are not enough. It's also vital that you take time to identify your Most Important Next Step (M.I.N.S.) for each goal, so your goal transforms into an action. And remember, when it comes to M.I.N.S., be specific.

Real Estate Goal: _____

Weekly Objective: _____

M.I.N.S. _____

Second Goal: _____

Weekly Objective: _____

M.I.N.S. _____

Third Goal: _____

Weekly Objective: _____

M.I.N.S. _____

I can consider today a "win" if I _____

Now, go place this on your time-blocking calendar for today.

REAL ESTATE L.A.P.S. FUNNEL

Use this space to set a daily goal for defining how you'll get **leads**, how many properties you'll **analyze**, how many properties you'll **pursue** (offer), and how many you'll **purchase** today.

GOAL   REALITY

LEADS

ANALYZE

PURSUE

$

TODAY'S TIME-BLOCKING ACTIVITIES

High-achieving real estate investors know that what gets scheduled gets done.
Take a few minutes to think about your goals, your M.I.N.S., and schedule your day.
Don't forget to include several breaks.

5AM–6AM _____   2PM–3PM _____

6AM–7AM _____   3PM–4PM _____

7AM–8AM _____   4PM–5PM _____

8AM–9AM _____   5PM–6PM _____

9AM–10AM _____   6PM–7PM _____

10AM–11AM _____   7PM–8PM _____

11AM–12PM _____   8PM–9PM _____

12PM–1PM _____   9PM–10PM _____

1PM–2PM _____   10PM–11PM _____

☐ Did I include enough breaks   ☐ Did I schedule my #1 most
    in the day?   important thing?

EVENING REVIEW

Today was awesome because _____

_____

Today I struggled with _____

_____

On a scale of 1–10, with 10 being the highest, I would rate today's
productivity at a...   1 2 3 4 5 6 7 8 9 10

Tomorrow I will...   Other Thoughts/Notes

_____   _____

_____   _____

_____   _____

_____   _____

_____   _____

_____   _____

DAILY ACTION PLAN

Date: ___ / ___ / ___

S M T W Th F S

"What you do today can improve all your tomorrows."
—Ralph Marston

MORNING ROUTINE

Wake-up time _____ Water ☐ Exercise ☐ Daily Journal ☐ _____ ☐

This morning, I'm grateful for _____

GOALS AND M.I.N.S.

Goals are important to review daily, reinforcing your objectives to your conscious and subconscious mind. But goals alone are not enough. It's also vital that you take time to identify your Most Important Next Step (M.I.N.S.) for each goal, so your goal transforms into an action. And remember, when it comes to M.I.N.S., be specific.

Real Estate Goal: _____

Weekly Objective: _____

M.I.N.S. _____

Second Goal: _____

Weekly Objective: _____

M.I.N.S. _____

Third Goal: _____

Weekly Objective: _____

M.I.N.S. _____

I can consider today a "win" if I _____

Now, go place this on your time-blocking calendar for today.

REAL ESTATE L.A.P.S. FUNNEL

Use this space to set a daily goal for defining how you'll get **leads**, how many properties you'll **analyze**, how many properties you'll **pursue** (offer), and how many you'll **purchase** today.

GOAL   REALITY

LEADS

ANALYZE

PURSUE

$

TODAY'S TIME-BLOCKING ACTIVITIES

High-achieving real estate investors know that what gets scheduled gets done.
Take a few minutes to think about your goals, your M.I.N.S., and schedule your day.
Don't forget to include several breaks.

5AM–6AM _____	2PM–3PM _____
6AM–7AM _____	3PM–4PM _____
7AM–8AM _____	4PM–5PM _____
8AM–9AM _____	5PM–6PM _____
9AM–10AM _____	6PM–7PM _____
10AM–11AM _____	7PM–8PM _____
11AM–12PM _____	8PM–9PM _____
12PM–1PM _____	9PM–10PM _____
1PM–2PM _____	10PM–11PM _____

☐ Did I include enough breaks in the day?

☐ Did I schedule my #1 most important thing?

EVENING REVIEW

Today was awesome because _____

_____

Today I struggled with _____

_____

On a scale of 1–10, with 10 being the highest, I would rate today's
productivity at a...   1 2 3 4 5 6 7 8 9 10

Tomorrow I will...   Other Thoughts/Notes

DAILY ACTION PLAN

Date: ____ / ____ / ____

S M T W Th F S

MORNING ROUTINE

Wake-up time _____   Water ☐   Exercise ☐   Daily Journal ☐   _____ ☐

This morning, I'm grateful for _____

GOALS AND M.I.N.S.

Goals are important to review daily, reinforcing your objectives to your conscious and subconscious mind. But goals alone are not enough. It's also vital that you take time to identify your Most Important Next Step (M.I.N.S.) for each goal, so your goal transforms into an action. And remember, when it comes to M.I.N.S., be specific.

Real Estate Goal: _____

Weekly Objective: _____

M.I.N.S. _____

Second Goal: _____

Weekly Objective: _____

M.I.N.S. _____

Third Goal: _____

Weekly Objective: _____

M.I.N.S. _____

I can consider today a "win" if I _____

Now, go place this on your time-blocking calendar for today.

REAL ESTATE L.A.P.S. FUNNEL

Use this space to set a daily goal for defining how you'll get **leads**, how many properties you'll **analyze**, how many properties you'll **pursue** (offer), and how many you'll **purchase** today.

GOAL   REALITY

LEADS

ANALYZE

PURSUE

$

TODAY'S TIME-BLOCKING ACTIVITIES

High-achieving real estate investors know that what gets scheduled gets done.
Take a few minutes to think about your goals, your M.I.N.S., and schedule your day.
Don't forget to include several breaks.

5AM–6AM _____	2PM–3PM _____
6AM–7AM _____	3PM–4PM _____
7AM–8AM _____	4PM–5PM _____
8AM–9AM _____	5PM–6PM _____
9AM–10AM _____	6PM–7PM _____
10AM–11AM _____	7PM–8PM _____
11AM–12PM _____	8PM–9PM _____
12PM–1PM _____	9PM–10PM _____
1PM–2PM _____	10PM–11PM _____

☐ Did I include enough breaks in the day?

☐ Did I schedule my #1 most important thing?

EVENING REVIEW

Today was awesome because _____

_____

Today I struggled with _____

_____

On a scale of 1–10, with 10 being the highest, I would rate today's
productivity at a...   1 2 3 4 5 6 7 8 9 10

Tomorrow I will...   Other Thoughts/Notes

_____   _____

_____   _____

_____   _____

_____   _____

_____   _____

_____   _____

DAILY ACTION PLAN

Date: ____ / ____ / ____

S M T W Th F S

"Either you run the day or the day runs you."
—Jim Rohn

MORNING ROUTINE

Wake-up time _____   Water ☐   Exercise ☐   Daily Journal ☐   _____ ☐

This morning, I'm grateful for _____

GOALS AND M.I.N.S.

Goals are important to review daily, reinforcing your objectives to your conscious and subconscious mind. But goals alone are not enough. It's also vital that you take time to identify your Most Important Next Step (M.I.N.S.) for each goal, so your goal transforms into an action. And remember, when it comes to M.I.N.S., be specific.

Real Estate Goal: _____

Weekly Objective: _____

M.I.N.S. _____

Second Goal: _____

Weekly Objective: _____

M.I.N.S. _____

Third Goal: _____

Weekly Objective: _____

M.I.N.S. _____

I can consider today a "win" if I _____

Now, go place this on your time-blocking calendar for today.

REAL ESTATE L.A.P.S. FUNNEL

Use this space to set a daily goal for defining how you'll get **leads**, how many properties you'll **analyze**, how many properties you'll **pursue** (offer), and how many you'll **purchase** today.

GOAL

REALITY

LEADS

ANALYZE

PURSUE

$

TODAY'S TIME-BLOCKING ACTIVITIES

High-achieving real estate investors know that what gets scheduled gets done.
Take a few minutes to think about your goals, your M.I.N.S., and schedule your day.
Don't forget to include several breaks.

5AM–6AM _____	2PM–3PM _____
6AM–7AM _____	3PM–4PM _____
7AM–8AM _____	4PM–5PM _____
8AM–9AM _____	5PM–6PM _____
9AM–10AM _____	6PM–7PM _____
10AM–11AM _____	7PM–8PM _____
11AM–12PM _____	8PM–9PM _____
12PM–1PM _____	9PM–10PM _____
1PM–2PM _____	10PM–11PM _____

☐ Did I include enough breaks in the day?

☐ Did I schedule my #1 most important thing?

EVENING REVIEW

Today was awesome because _____

_____

Today I struggled with _____

_____

On a scale of 1–10, with 10 being the highest, I would rate today's
productivity at a...   1   2   3   4   5   6   7   8   9   10

Tomorrow I will...

Other Thoughts/Notes

DAILY ACTION PLAN

Date: ___ / ___ / ___   S M T W Th F S

"By failing to prepare, you are preparing to fail."
—Benjamin Franklin

MORNING ROUTINE

Wake-up time _____ Water ☐ Exercise ☐ Daily Journal ☐ _____ ☐

This morning, I'm grateful for _____

GOALS AND M.I.N.S.

Goals are important to review daily, reinforcing your objectives to your conscious and subconscious mind. But goals alone are not enough. It's also vital that you take time to identify your Most Important Next Step (M.I.N.S.) for each goal, so your goal transforms into an action. And remember, when it comes to M.I.N.S., be specific.

Real Estate Goal: _____

Weekly Objective: _____

M.I.N.S. _____

Second Goal: _____

Weekly Objective: _____

M.I.N.S. _____

Third Goal: _____

Weekly Objective: _____

M.I.N.S. _____

I can consider today a "win" if I _____

Now, go place this on your time-blocking calendar for today.

REAL ESTATE L.A.P.S. FUNNEL

Use this space to set a daily goal for defining how you'll get **leads**, how many properties you'll **analyze**, how many properties you'll **pursue** (offer), and how many you'll **purchase** today.

GOAL   REALITY

LEADS

ANALYZE

PURSUE

$

TODAY'S TIME-BLOCKING ACTIVITIES

High-achieving real estate investors know that what gets scheduled gets done.
Take a few minutes to think about your goals, your M.I.N.S., and schedule your day.
Don't forget to include several breaks.

5AM–6AM	_____	2PM–3PM	_____
6AM–7AM	_____	3PM–4PM	_____
7AM–8AM	_____	4PM–5PM	_____
8AM–9AM	_____	5PM–6PM	_____
9AM–10AM	_____	6PM–7PM	_____
10AM–11AM	_____	7PM–8PM	_____
11AM–12PM	_____	8PM–9PM	_____
12PM–1PM	_____	9PM–10PM	_____
1PM–2PM	_____	10PM–11PM	_____

☐ Did I include enough breaks in the day?

☐ Did I schedule my #1 most important thing?

EVENING REVIEW

Today was awesome because _____

_____

Today I struggled with _____

_____

On a scale of 1–10, with 10 being the highest, I would rate today's
productivity at a...   1 2 3 4 5 6 7 8 9 10

Tomorrow I will...

_____

_____

_____

_____

_____

_____

Other Thoughts/Notes

_____

_____

_____

_____

_____

_____

Date: ____ / ____ / ____   # DAILY ACTION PLAN   S M T W Th F S

"The true test of leadership is how well you function in a crisis."
—Brian Tracy

MORNING ROUTINE

Wake-up time _____   Water ☐   Exercise ☐   Daily Journal ☐   _____ ☐

This morning, I'm grateful for _____

GOALS AND M.I.N.S.

Goals are important to review daily, reinforcing your objectives to your conscious and subconscious mind. But goals alone are not enough. It's also vital that you take time to identify your Most Important Next Step (M.I.N.S.) for each goal, so your goal transforms into an action. And remember, when it comes to M.I.N.S., be specific.

Real Estate Goal: _____

Weekly Objective: _____

M.I.N.S. _____

Second Goal: _____

Weekly Objective: _____

M.I.N.S. _____

Third Goal: _____

Weekly Objective: _____

M.I.N.S. _____

I can consider today a "win" if I _____

Now, go place this on your time-blocking calendar for today.

REAL ESTATE L.A.P.S. FUNNEL

Use this space to set a daily goal for defining how you'll get **leads**, how many properties you'll **analyze**, how many properties you'll **pursue** (offer), and how many you'll **purchase** today.

GOAL   REALITY

LEADS

ANALYZE

PURSUE

$

TODAY'S TIME-BLOCKING ACTIVITIES

High-achieving real estate investors know that what gets scheduled gets done.
Take a few minutes to think about your goals, your M.I.N.S., and schedule your day.
Don't forget to include several breaks.

5AM–6AM	_____	2PM–3PM	_____
6AM–7AM	_____	3PM–4PM	_____
7AM–8AM	_____	4PM–5PM	_____
8AM–9AM	_____	5PM–6PM	_____
9AM–10AM	_____	6PM–7PM	_____
10AM–11AM	_____	7PM–8PM	_____
11AM–12PM	_____	8PM–9PM	_____
12PM–1PM	_____	9PM–10PM	_____
1PM–2PM	_____	10PM–11PM	_____

☐ Did I include enough breaks in the day?

☐ Did I schedule my #1 most important thing?

EVENING REVIEW

Today was awesome because _____

_____

Today I struggled with _____

_____

On a scale of 1–10, with 10 being the highest, I would rate today's productivity at a...   1   2   3   4   5   6   7   8   9   10

Tomorrow I will...

Other Thoughts/Notes

DAILY ACTION PLAN

Date: ____ / ____ / ____   S M T W Th F S

"Believe you can and you're halfway there."
—THEODORE ROOSEVELT

MORNING ROUTINE

Wake-up time _____   Water ☐   Exercise ☐   Daily Journal ☐   _____ ☐

This morning, I'm grateful for _____

GOALS AND M.I.N.S.

Goals are important to review daily, reinforcing your objectives to your conscious and subconscious mind. But goals alone are not enough. It's also vital that you take time to identify your Most Important Next Step (M.I.N.S.) for each goal, so your goal transforms into an action. And remember, when it comes to M.I.N.S., be specific.

Real Estate Goal: _____

Weekly Objective: _____

M.I.N.S. _____

Second Goal: _____

Weekly Objective: _____

M.I.N.S. _____

Third Goal: _____

Weekly Objective: _____

M.I.N.S. _____

I can consider today a "win" if I _____

Now, go place this on your time-blocking calendar for today.

REAL ESTATE L.A.P.S. FUNNEL

Use this space to set a daily goal for defining how you'll get **leads**, how many properties you'll **analyze**, how many properties you'll **pursue** (offer), and how many you'll **purchase** today.

GOAL   REALITY

LEADS
_____   _____

ANALYZE
_____   _____

PURSUE
_____   _____

$
_____   _____

TODAY'S TIME-BLOCKING ACTIVITIES

High-achieving real estate investors know that what gets scheduled gets done.
Take a few minutes to think about your goals, your M.I.N.S., and schedule your day.
Don't forget to include several breaks.

5AM–6AM _____	2PM–3PM _____
6AM–7AM _____	3PM–4PM _____
7AM–8AM _____	4PM–5PM _____
8AM–9AM _____	5PM–6PM _____
9AM–10AM _____	6PM–7PM _____
10AM–11AM _____	7PM–8PM _____
11AM–12PM _____	8PM–9PM _____
12PM–1PM _____	9PM–10PM _____
1PM–2PM _____	10PM–11PM _____

☐ Did I include enough breaks in the day?

☐ Did I schedule my #1 most important thing?

EVENING REVIEW

Today was awesome because _____

_____

Today I struggled with _____

_____

On a scale of 1–10, with 10 being the highest, I would rate today's
productivity at a...   1   2   3   4   5   6   7   8   9   10

Tomorrow I will...   Other Thoughts/Notes

Date: ____ / ____ / ____ # DAILY ACTION PLAN

*"If my mind can conceive it and my heart can believe it—
then I can achieve it."*
—Muhammad Ali

MORNING ROUTINE

Wake-up time _____ Water ☐ Exercise ☐ Daily Journal ☐ _____ ☐

This morning, I'm grateful for _____

GOALS AND M.I.N.S.

*Goals are important to review daily, reinforcing your objectives to your conscious and
subconscious mind. But goals alone are not enough. It's also vital that you take time to
identify your Most Important Next Step (M.I.N.S.) for each goal, so your goal transforms
into an action. And remember, when it comes to M.I.N.S., be specific.*

Real Estate Goal: _____

Weekly Objective: _____

M.I.N.S. _____

Second Goal: _____

Weekly Objective: _____

M.I.N.S. _____

Third Goal: _____

Weekly Objective: _____

M.I.N.S. _____

I can consider today a "win" if I _____

Now, go place this on your time-blocking calendar for today.

REAL ESTATE L.A.P.S. FUNNEL

GOAL   REALITY

Use this space to set a daily goal for
defining how you'll get **leads**, how many
properties you'll **analyze**, how many
properties you'll **pursue** (offer), and how
many you'll **purchase** today.

LEADS

ANALYZE

PURSUE

$

TODAY'S TIME-BLOCKING ACTIVITIES

High-achieving real estate investors know that what gets scheduled gets done.
Take a few minutes to think about your goals, your M.I.N.S., and schedule your day.
Don't forget to include several breaks.

5AM–6AM _____	2PM–3PM _____
6AM–7AM _____	3PM–4PM _____
7AM–8AM _____	4PM–5PM _____
8AM–9AM _____	5PM–6PM _____
9AM–10AM _____	6PM–7PM _____
10AM–11AM _____	7PM–8PM _____
11AM–12PM _____	8PM–9PM _____
12PM–1PM _____	9PM–10PM _____
1PM–2PM _____	10PM–11PM _____

☐ Did I include enough breaks in the day?

☐ Did I schedule my #1 most important thing?

EVENING REVIEW

Today was awesome because _____

_____

Today I struggled with _____

_____

On a scale of 1–10, with 10 being the highest, I would rate today's
productivity at a...   1 2 3 4 5 6 7 8 9 10

Tomorrow I will...   Other Thoughts/Notes

Date: ___ / ___ / ___ # DAILY ACTION PLAN S M T W Th F S

"Do. Or do not. There is no try."
—MASTER YODA

MORNING ROUTINE

Wake-up time _____ Water ☐ Exercise ☐ Daily Journal ☐ _____ ☐

This morning, I'm grateful for _____

GOALS AND M.I.N.S.

Goals are important to review daily, reinforcing your objectives to your conscious and subconscious mind. But goals alone are not enough. It's also vital that you take time to identify your Most Important Next Step (M.I.N.S.) for each goal, so your goal transforms into an action. And remember, when it comes to M.I.N.S., be specific.

Real Estate Goal: _____

Weekly Objective: _____

M.I.N.S. _____

Second Goal: _____

Weekly Objective: _____

M.I.N.S. _____

Third Goal: _____

Weekly Objective: _____

M.I.N.S. _____

I can consider today a "win" if I _____

Now, go place this on your time-blocking calendar for today.

REAL ESTATE L.A.P.S. FUNNEL

Use this space to set a daily goal for defining how you'll get **leads**, how many properties you'll **analyze**, how many properties you'll **pursue** (offer), and how many you'll **purchase** today.

GOAL   REALITY

LEADS

ANALYZE

PURSUE

$

TODAY'S TIME-BLOCKING ACTIVITIES

High-achieving real estate investors know that what gets scheduled gets done.
Take a few minutes to think about your goals, your M.I.N.S., and schedule your day.
Don't forget to include several breaks.

5AM–6AM _____	2PM–3PM _____
6AM–7AM _____	3PM–4PM _____
7AM–8AM _____	4PM–5PM _____
8AM–9AM _____	5PM–6PM _____
9AM–10AM _____	6PM–7PM _____
10AM–11AM _____	7PM–8PM _____
11AM–12PM _____	8PM–9PM _____
12PM–1PM _____	9PM–10PM _____
1PM–2PM _____	10PM–11PM _____

☐ Did I include enough breaks in the day?

☐ Did I schedule my #1 most important thing?

EVENING REVIEW

Today was awesome because _____

_____

Today I struggled with _____

_____

On a scale of 1–10, with 10 being the highest, I would rate today's
productivity at a...   1   2   3   4   5   6   7   8   9   10

Tomorrow I will...

Other Thoughts/Notes

Date: ___ / ___ / ___   # DAILY ACTION PLAN   S M T W Th F S

MORNING ROUTINE

Wake-up time _____   Water ☐   Exercise ☐   Daily Journal ☐   _____ ☐

This morning, I'm grateful for _____

GOALS AND M.I.N.S.

*Goals are important to review daily, reinforcing your objectives to your conscious and
subconscious mind. But goals alone are not enough. It's also vital that you take time to
identify your Most Important Next Step (M.I.N.S.) for each goal, so your goal transforms
into an action. And remember, when it comes to M.I.N.S., be specific.*

Real Estate Goal: _____

Weekly Objective: _____

M.I.N.S. _____

Second Goal: _____

Weekly Objective: _____

M.I.N.S. _____

Third Goal: _____

Weekly Objective: _____

M.I.N.S. _____

I can consider today a "win" if I _____

Now, go place this on your time-blocking calendar for today.

REAL ESTATE L.A.P.S. FUNNEL

Use this space to set a daily goal for
defining how you'll get **leads**, how many
properties you'll **analyze**, how many
properties you'll **pursue** (offer), and how
many you'll **purchase** today.

GOAL   REALITY

LEADS

ANALYZE

PURSUE

$

TODAY'S TIME-BLOCKING ACTIVITIES

High-achieving real estate investors know that what gets scheduled gets done.
Take a few minutes to think about your goals, your M.I.N.S., and schedule your day.
Don't forget to include several breaks.

5AM–6AM ———————————   2PM–3PM ———————————

6AM–7AM ———————————   3PM–4PM ———————————

7AM–8AM ———————————   4PM–5PM ———————————

8AM–9AM ———————————   5PM–6PM ———————————

9AM–10AM ——————————   6PM–7PM ———————————

10AM–11AM —————————   7PM–8PM ———————————

11AM–12PM —————————   8PM–9PM ———————————

12PM–1PM ———————————   9PM–10PM ——————————

1PM–2PM ———————————   10PM–11PM —————————

☐ Did I include enough breaks in the day?   ☐ Did I schedule my #1 most important thing?

EVENING REVIEW

Today was awesome because ———————————————————————

——

Today I struggled with ——————————————————————————

——

On a scale of 1–10, with 10 being the highest, I would rate today's
productivity at a...   1 2 3 4 5 6 7 8 9 10

Tomorrow I will...   Other Thoughts/Notes

DAILY ACTION PLAN

Date: ____ / ____ / ____   S M T W Th F S

*"I can accept failure, everyone fails at something.
But I can't accept not trying."*
—MICHAEL JORDAN

MORNING ROUTINE

Wake-up time _____   Water ☐   Exercise ☐   Daily Journal ☐   _____ ☐

This morning, I'm grateful for _____

GOALS AND M.I.N.S.

Goals are important to review daily, reinforcing your objectives to your conscious and subconscious mind. But goals alone are not enough. It's also vital that you take time to identify your Most Important Next Step (M.I.N.S.) for each goal, so your goal transforms into an action. And remember, when it comes to M.I.N.S., be specific.

Real Estate Goal: _____

Weekly Objective: _____

M.I.N.S. _____

Second Goal: _____

Weekly Objective: _____

M.I.N.S. _____

Third Goal: _____

Weekly Objective: _____

M.I.N.S. _____

I can consider today a "win" if I _____

Now, go place this on your time-blocking calendar for today.

REAL ESTATE L.A.P.S. FUNNEL

Use this space to set a daily goal for defining how you'll get **leads**, how many properties you'll **analyze**, how many properties you'll **pursue** (offer), and how many you'll **purchase** today.

GOAL   REALITY

LEADS

ANALYZE

PURSUE

$

TODAY'S TIME-BLOCKING ACTIVITIES

High-achieving real estate investors know that what gets scheduled gets done.
Take a few minutes to think about your goals, your M.I.N.S., and schedule your day.
Don't forget to include several breaks.

5AM–6AM _____   2PM–3PM _____

6AM–7AM _____   3PM–4PM _____

7AM–8AM _____   4PM–5PM _____

8AM–9AM _____   5PM–6PM _____

9AM–10AM _____   6PM–7PM _____

10AM–11AM _____   7PM–8PM _____

11AM–12PM _____   8PM–9PM _____

12PM–1PM _____   9PM–10PM _____

1PM–2PM _____   10PM–11PM _____

☐ Did I include enough breaks   ☐ Did I schedule my #1 most
   in the day?   important thing?

EVENING REVIEW

Today was awesome because _____

_____

Today I struggled with _____

_____

On a scale of 1–10, with 10 being the highest, I would rate today's
productivity at a...   1   2   3   4   5   6   7   8   9   10

Tomorrow I will...   Other Thoughts/Notes

_____   _____

_____   _____

_____   _____

_____   _____

_____   _____

_____   _____

DAILY ACTION PLAN

Date: ____ / ____ / ____

S M T W Th F S

MORNING ROUTINE

Wake-up time _____ Water ☐ Exercise ☐ Daily Journal ☐ _____ ☐

This morning, I'm grateful for _____

GOALS AND M.I.N.S.

Goals are important to review daily, reinforcing your objectives to your conscious and subconscious mind. But goals alone are not enough. It's also vital that you take time to identify your Most Important Next Step (M.I.N.S.) for each goal, so your goal transforms into an action. And remember, when it comes to M.I.N.S., be specific.

Real Estate Goal: _____

Weekly Objective: _____

M.I.N.S. _____

Second Goal: _____

Weekly Objective: _____

M.I.N.S. _____

Third Goal: _____

Weekly Objective: _____

M.I.N.S. _____

I can consider today a "win" if I _____

Now, go place this on your time-blocking calendar for today.

REAL ESTATE L.A.P.S. FUNNEL

Use this space to set a daily goal for defining how you'll get **leads**, how many properties you'll **analyze**, how many properties you'll **pursue** (offer), and how many you'll **purchase** today.

GOAL

REALITY

LEADS

ANALYZE

PURSUE

$

TODAY'S TIME-BLOCKING ACTIVITIES

High-achieving real estate investors know that what gets scheduled gets done.
Take a few minutes to think about your goals, your M.I.N.S., and schedule your day.
Don't forget to include several breaks.

5AM–6AM	_____	2PM–3PM	_____
6AM–7AM	_____	3PM–4PM	_____
7AM–8AM	_____	4PM–5PM	_____
8AM–9AM	_____	5PM–6PM	_____
9AM–10AM	_____	6PM–7PM	_____
10AM–11AM	_____	7PM–8PM	_____
11AM–12PM	_____	8PM–9PM	_____
12PM–1PM	_____	9PM–10PM	_____
1PM–2PM	_____	10PM–11PM	_____

☐ Did I include enough breaks in the day?

☐ Did I schedule my #1 most important thing?

EVENING REVIEW

Today was awesome because _____

_____

Today I struggled with _____

_____

On a scale of 1–10, with 10 being the highest, I would rate today's
productivity at a...   1 2 3 4 5 6 7 8 9 10

Tomorrow I will...   Other Thoughts/Notes

_____   _____

_____   _____

_____   _____

_____   _____

_____   _____

_____   _____

DAILY ACTION PLAN

Date: ____ / ____ / ____

S M T W Th F S

MORNING ROUTINE

Wake-up time _____ Water ☐ Exercise ☐ Daily Journal ☐ _____ ☐

This morning, I'm grateful for _____

GOALS AND M.I.N.S.

Goals are important to review daily, reinforcing your objectives to your conscious and subconscious mind. But goals alone are not enough. It's also vital that you take time to identify your Most Important Next Step (M.I.N.S.) for each goal, so your goal transforms into an action. And remember, when it comes to M.I.N.S., be specific.

Real Estate Goal: _____

Weekly Objective: _____

M.I.N.S. _____

Second Goal: _____

Weekly Objective: _____

M.I.N.S. _____

Third Goal: _____

Weekly Objective: _____

M.I.N.S. _____

I can consider today a "win" if I _____

Now, go place this on your time-blocking calendar for today.

REAL ESTATE L.A.P.S. FUNNEL

Use this space to set a daily goal for defining how you'll get **leads**, how many properties you'll **analyze**, how many properties you'll **pursue** (offer), and how many you'll **purchase** today.

GOAL   REALITY

LEADS

ANALYZE

PURSUE

$

TODAY'S TIME-BLOCKING ACTIVITIES

High-achieving real estate investors know that what gets scheduled gets done.
Take a few minutes to think about your goals, your M.I.N.S., and schedule your day.
Don't forget to include several breaks.

5AM–6AM _____

6AM–7AM _____

7AM–8AM _____

8AM–9AM _____

9AM–10AM _____

10AM–11AM _____

11AM–12PM _____

12PM–1PM _____

1PM–2PM _____

2PM–3PM _____

3PM–4PM _____

4PM–5PM _____

5PM–6PM _____

6PM–7PM _____

7PM–8PM _____

8PM–9PM _____

9PM–10PM _____

10PM–11PM _____

☐ Did I include enough breaks in the day?

☐ Did I schedule my #1 most important thing?

EVENING REVIEW

Today was awesome because _____

_____

Today I struggled with _____

_____

On a scale of 1–10, with 10 being the highest, I would rate today's
productivity at a...   1 2 3 4 5 6 7 8 9 10

Tomorrow I will...

_____

_____

_____

_____

_____

_____

Other Thoughts/Notes

_____

_____

_____

_____

_____

_____

DAILY ACTION PLAN

Date: ___ / ___ / ___   S M T W Th F S

"The most difficult thing is the decision to act,
the rest is merely tenacity."

—AMELIA EARHART

MORNING ROUTINE

Wake-up time _____   Water ☐   Exercise ☐   Daily Journal ☐   _____ ☐

This morning, I'm grateful for _____

GOALS AND M.I.N.S.

Goals are important to review daily, reinforcing your objectives to your conscious and subconscious mind. But goals alone are not enough. It's also vital that you take time to identify your Most Important Next Step (M.I.N.S.) for each goal, so your goal transforms into an action. And remember, when it comes to M.I.N.S., be specific.

Real Estate Goal: _____

Weekly Objective: _____

M.I.N.S. _____

Second Goal: _____

Weekly Objective: _____

M.I.N.S. _____

Third Goal: _____

Weekly Objective: _____

M.I.N.S. _____

I can consider today a "win" if I _____

Now, go place this on your time-blocking calendar for today.

REAL ESTATE L.A.P.S. FUNNEL

Use this space to set a daily goal for defining how you'll get **leads**, how many properties you'll **analyze**, how many properties you'll **pursue** (offer), and how many you'll **purchase** today.

GOAL   REALITY

LEADS

ANALYZE

PURSUE

$

TODAY'S TIME-BLOCKING ACTIVITIES

High-achieving real estate investors know that what gets scheduled gets done.
Take a few minutes to think about your goals, your M.I.N.S., and schedule your day.
Don't forget to include several breaks.

5AM–6AM _____	2PM–3PM _____
6AM–7AM _____	3PM–4PM _____
7AM–8AM _____	4PM–5PM _____
8AM–9AM _____	5PM–6PM _____
9AM–10AM _____	6PM–7PM _____
10AM–11AM _____	7PM–8PM _____
11AM–12PM _____	8PM–9PM _____
12PM–1PM _____	9PM–10PM _____
1PM–2PM _____	10PM–11PM _____

☐ Did I include enough breaks in the day?

☐ Did I schedule my #1 most important thing?

EVENING REVIEW

Today was awesome because _____

_____

Today I struggled with _____

_____

On a scale of 1–10, with 10 being the highest, I would rate today's
productivity at a...   1 2 3 4 5 6 7 8 9 10

Tomorrow I will...   Other Thoughts/Notes

_____   _____

_____   _____

_____   _____

_____   _____

_____   _____

_____   _____

Date: ____ / ____ / ____ # DAILY ACTION PLAN S M T W Th F S

"Done is better than perfect."
—SHERYL SANDBERG

MORNING ROUTINE

Wake-up time _____ Water ☐ Exercise ☐ Daily Journal ☐ _____ ☐

This morning, I'm grateful for _____

GOALS AND M.I.N.S.

Goals are important to review daily, reinforcing your objectives to your conscious and subconscious mind. But goals alone are not enough. It's also vital that you take time to identify your Most Important Next Step (M.I.N.S.) for each goal, so your goal transforms into an action. And remember, when it comes to M.I.N.S., be specific.

Real Estate Goal: _____

Weekly Objective: _____

M.I.N.S. _____

Second Goal: _____

Weekly Objective: _____

M.I.N.S. _____

Third Goal: _____

Weekly Objective: _____

M.I.N.S. _____

I can consider today a "win" if I _____

Now, go place this on your time-blocking calendar for today.

REAL ESTATE L.A.P.S. FUNNEL

Use this space to set a daily goal for defining how you'll get **leads**, how many properties you'll **analyze**, how many properties you'll **pursue** (offer), and how many you'll **purchase** today.

GOAL   REALITY

LEADS

ANALYZE

PURSUE

$

TODAY'S TIME-BLOCKING ACTIVITIES

High-achieving real estate investors know that what gets scheduled gets done.
Take a few minutes to think about your goals, your M.I.N.S., and schedule your day.
Don't forget to include several breaks.

5AM–6AM _____   2PM–3PM _____

6AM–7AM _____   3PM–4PM _____

7AM–8AM _____   4PM–5PM _____

8AM–9AM _____   5PM–6PM _____

9AM–10AM _____   6PM–7PM _____

10AM–11AM _____   7PM–8PM _____

11AM–12PM _____   8PM–9PM _____

12PM–1PM _____   9PM–10PM _____

1PM–2PM _____   10PM–11PM _____

☐ Did I include enough breaks   ☐ Did I schedule my #1 most
   in the day?   important thing?

EVENING REVIEW

Today was awesome because _____

_____

Today I struggled with _____

_____

On a scale of 1–10, with 10 being the highest, I would rate today's
productivity at a...   1   2   3   4   5   6   7   8   9   10

Tomorrow I will...   Other Thoughts/Notes

_____   _____

_____   _____

_____   _____

_____   _____

_____   _____

_____   _____

_____   _____

DAILY ACTION PLAN

Date: ____ / ____ / ____

S M T W Th F S

"Fake it until you make it! Act as if you had all the confidence you require until it becomes your reality."

—Brian Tracy

MORNING ROUTINE

Wake-up time _____ Water ☐ Exercise ☐ Daily Journal ☐ _____ ☐

This morning, I'm grateful for _____

GOALS AND M.I.N.S.

Goals are important to review daily, reinforcing your objectives to your conscious and subconscious mind. But goals alone are not enough. It's also vital that you take time to identify your Most Important Next Step (M.I.N.S.) for each goal, so your goal transforms into an action. And remember, when it comes to M.I.N.S., be specific.

Real Estate Goal: _____

Weekly Objective: _____

M.I.N.S. _____

Second Goal: _____

Weekly Objective: _____

M.I.N.S. _____

Third Goal: _____

Weekly Objective: _____

M.I.N.S. _____

I can consider today a "win" if I _____

Now, go place this on your time-blocking calendar for today.

REAL ESTATE L.A.P.S. FUNNEL

Use this space to set a daily goal for defining how you'll get **leads**, how many properties you'll **analyze**, how many properties you'll **pursue** (offer), and how many you'll **purchase** today.

GOAL

REALITY

LEADS

ANALYZE

PURSUE

$

TODAY'S TIME-BLOCKING ACTIVITIES

High-achieving real estate investors know that what gets scheduled gets done.
Take a few minutes to think about your goals, your M.I.N.S., and schedule your day.
Don't forget to include several breaks.

5AM–6AM	_____	2PM–3PM	_____
6AM–7AM	_____	3PM–4PM	_____
7AM–8AM	_____	4PM–5PM	_____
8AM–9AM	_____	5PM–6PM	_____
9AM–10AM	_____	6PM–7PM	_____
10AM–11AM	_____	7PM–8PM	_____
11AM–12PM	_____	8PM–9PM	_____
12PM–1PM	_____	9PM–10PM	_____
1PM–2PM	_____	10PM–11PM	_____

☐ Did I include enough breaks in the day?

☐ Did I schedule my #1 most important thing?

EVENING REVIEW

Today was awesome because _____

_____

Today I struggled with _____

_____

On a scale of 1–10, with 10 being the highest, I would rate today's productivity at a...   1 2 3 4 5 6 7 8 9 10

Tomorrow I will...

Other Thoughts/Notes

DAILY ACTION PLAN

Date: ____ / ____ / ____

S M T W Th F S

"No one changes the world who isn't obsessed."
—BILLIE JEAN KING

MORNING ROUTINE

Wake-up time _____ Water ☐ Exercise ☐ Daily Journal ☐ _____ ☐

This morning, I'm grateful for _____

GOALS AND M.I.N.S.

Goals are important to review daily, reinforcing your objectives to your conscious and subconscious mind. But goals alone are not enough. It's also vital that you take time to identify your Most Important Next Step (M.I.N.S.) for each goal, so your goal transforms into an action. And remember, when it comes to M.I.N.S., be specific.

Real Estate Goal: _____

Weekly Objective: _____

M.I.N.S. _____

Second Goal: _____

Weekly Objective: _____

M.I.N.S. _____

Third Goal: _____

Weekly Objective: _____

M.I.N.S. _____

I can consider today a "win" if I _____

Now, go place this on your time-blocking calendar for today.

REAL ESTATE L.A.P.S. FUNNEL

Use this space to set a daily goal for defining how you'll get **leads**, how many properties you'll **analyze**, how many properties you'll **pursue** (offer), and how many you'll **purchase** today.

GOAL

REALITY

LEADS

ANALYZE

PURSUE

$

TODAY'S TIME-BLOCKING ACTIVITIES

High-achieving real estate investors know that what gets scheduled gets done.
Take a few minutes to think about your goals, your M.I.N.S., and schedule your day.
Don't forget to include several breaks.

5AM–6AM	_____	2PM–3PM	_____
6AM–7AM	_____	3PM–4PM	_____
7AM–8AM	_____	4PM–5PM	_____
8AM–9AM	_____	5PM–6PM	_____
9AM–10AM	_____	6PM–7PM	_____
10AM–11AM	_____	7PM–8PM	_____
11AM–12PM	_____	8PM–9PM	_____
12PM–1PM	_____	9PM–10PM	_____
1PM–2PM	_____	10PM–11PM	_____

☐ Did I include enough breaks in the day?

☐ Did I schedule my #1 most important thing?

EVENING REVIEW

Today was awesome because _____

_____

Today I struggled with _____

_____

On a scale of 1–10, with 10 being the highest, I would rate today's
productivity at a...   1 2 3 4 5 6 7 8 9 10

Tomorrow I will...   Other Thoughts/Notes

_____   _____

_____   _____

_____   _____

_____   _____

_____   _____

_____   _____

DAILY ACTION PLAN

Date: ___ / ___ / ___   S M T W Th F S

MORNING ROUTINE

Wake-up time _____   Water ☐   Exercise ☐   Daily Journal ☐   _____ ☐

This morning, I'm grateful for _____

GOALS AND M.I.N.S.

Goals are important to review daily, reinforcing your objectives to your conscious and subconscious mind. But goals alone are not enough. It's also vital that you take time to identify your Most Important Next Step (M.I.N.S.) for each goal, so your goal transforms into an action. And remember, when it comes to M.I.N.S., be specific.

Real Estate Goal: _____

Weekly Objective: _____

M.I.N.S. _____

Second Goal: _____

Weekly Objective: _____

M.I.N.S. _____

Third Goal: _____

Weekly Objective: _____

M.I.N.S. _____

I can consider today a "win" if I _____

Now, go place this on your time-blocking calendar for today.

REAL ESTATE L.A.P.S. FUNNEL

GOAL   REALITY

Use this space to set a daily goal for defining how you'll get **leads**, how many properties you'll **analyze**, how many properties you'll **pursue** (offer), and how many you'll **purchase** today.

LEADS

ANALYZE

PURSUE

$

TODAY'S TIME-BLOCKING ACTIVITIES

High-achieving real estate investors know that what gets scheduled gets done.
Take a few minutes to think about your goals, your M.I.N.S., and schedule your day.
Don't forget to include several breaks.

5AM–6AM _____	2PM–3PM _____
6AM–7AM _____	3PM–4PM _____
7AM–8AM _____	4PM–5PM _____
8AM–9AM _____	5PM–6PM _____
9AM–10AM _____	6PM–7PM _____
10AM–11AM _____	7PM–8PM _____
11AM–12PM _____	8PM–9PM _____
12PM–1PM _____	9PM–10PM _____
1PM–2PM _____	10PM–11PM _____

☐ Did I include enough breaks in the day?

☐ Did I schedule my #1 most important thing?

EVENING REVIEW

Today was awesome because _____

_____

Today I struggled with _____

_____

On a scale of 1–10, with 10 being the highest, I would rate today's
productivity at a...   1   2   3   4   5   6   7   8   9   10

Tomorrow I will...

Other Thoughts/Notes

DAILY ACTION PLAN

Date: ____ / ____ / ____   S M T W Th F S

"The question isn't who is going to let me;
it's who is going to stop me."
—Ayn Rand

MORNING ROUTINE

Wake-up time _____   Water ☐   Exercise ☐   Daily Journal ☐   _____ ☐

This morning, I'm grateful for _____

GOALS AND M.I.N.S.

Goals are important to review daily, reinforcing your objectives to your conscious and
subconscious mind. But goals alone are not enough. It's also vital that you take time to
identify your Most Important Next Step (M.I.N.S.) for each goal, so your goal transforms
into an action. And remember, when it comes to M.I.N.S., be specific.

Real Estate Goal: _____

Weekly Objective: _____

M.I.N.S. _____

Second Goal: _____

Weekly Objective: _____

M.I.N.S. _____

Third Goal: _____

Weekly Objective: _____

M.I.N.S. _____

I can consider today a "win" if I _____

Now, go place this on your time-blocking calendar for today.

REAL ESTATE L.A.P.S. FUNNEL

Use this space to set a daily goal for
defining how you'll get **leads**, how many
properties you'll **analyze**, how many
properties you'll **pursue** (offer), and how
many you'll **purchase** today.

GOAL   REALITY

LEADS

ANALYZE

PURSUE

$

TODAY'S TIME-BLOCKING ACTIVITIES

High-achieving real estate investors know that what gets scheduled gets done.
Take a few minutes to think about your goals, your M.I.N.S., and schedule your day.
Don't forget to include several breaks.

5AM–6AM	_____	2PM–3PM	_____
6AM–7AM	_____	3PM–4PM	_____
7AM–8AM	_____	4PM–5PM	_____
8AM–9AM	_____	5PM–6PM	_____
9AM–10AM	_____	6PM–7PM	_____
10AM–11AM	_____	7PM–8PM	_____
11AM–12PM	_____	8PM–9PM	_____
12PM–1PM	_____	9PM–10PM	_____
1PM–2PM	_____	10PM–11PM	_____

☐ Did I include enough breaks in the day?

☐ Did I schedule my #1 most important thing?

EVENING REVIEW

Today was awesome because _____

_____

Today I struggled with _____

_____

On a scale of 1–10, with 10 being the highest, I would rate today's
productivity at a...   1   2   3   4   5   6   7   8   9   10

Tomorrow I will...   Other Thoughts/Notes

DAILY ACTION PLAN

Date: ____ / ____ / ____

S M T W Th F S

"Leaders think and talk about the solutions.
Followers think and talk about the problems."
—Brian Tracy

MORNING ROUTINE

Wake-up time _____ Water ☐ Exercise ☐ Daily Journal ☐ _____ ☐

This morning, I'm grateful for _____

GOALS AND M.I.N.S.

Goals are important to review daily, reinforcing your objectives to your conscious and subconscious mind. But goals alone are not enough. It's also vital that you take time to identify your Most Important Next Step (M.I.N.S.) for each goal, so your goal transforms into an action. And remember, when it comes to M.I.N.S., be specific.

Real Estate Goal: _____

Weekly Objective: _____

M.I.N.S. _____

Second Goal: _____

Weekly Objective: _____

M.I.N.S. _____

Third Goal: _____

Weekly Objective: _____

M.I.N.S. _____

I can consider today a "win" if I _____

Now, go place this on your time-blocking calendar for today.

REAL ESTATE L.A.P.S. FUNNEL

Use this space to set a daily goal for defining how you'll get **leads**, how many properties you'll **analyze**, how many properties you'll **pursue** (offer), and how many you'll **purchase** today.

GOAL   REALITY

LEADS

ANALYZE

PURSUE

$

TODAY'S TIME-BLOCKING ACTIVITIES

High-achieving real estate investors know that what gets scheduled gets done.
Take a few minutes to think about your goals, your M.I.N.S., and schedule your day.
Don't forget to include several breaks.

5AM–6AM _____	2PM–3PM _____
6AM–7AM _____	3PM–4PM _____
7AM–8AM _____	4PM–5PM _____
8AM–9AM _____	5PM–6PM _____
9AM–10AM _____	6PM–7PM _____
10AM–11AM _____	7PM–8PM _____
11AM–12PM _____	8PM–9PM _____
12PM–1PM _____	9PM–10PM _____
1PM–2PM _____	10PM–11PM _____

☐ Did I include enough breaks in the day?

☐ Did I schedule my #1 most important thing?

EVENING REVIEW

Today was awesome because _____

_____

Today I struggled with _____

_____

On a scale of 1–10, with 10 being the highest, I would rate today's
productivity at a...   1 2 3 4 5 6 7 8 9 10

Tomorrow I will...   Other Thoughts/Notes

_____   _____

_____   _____

_____   _____

_____   _____

_____   _____

_____   _____

DAILY ACTION PLAN

Date: ____ / ____ / ____   S M T W Th F S

The greatest challenge of the day is: how to bring about a revolution
of the heart, a revolution which has to start with each one of us?
—DOROTHY DAY

MORNING ROUTINE

Wake-up time _____ Water ☐ Exercise ☐ Daily Journal ☐ _____ ☐

This morning, I'm grateful for _____

GOALS AND M.I.N.S.

Goals are important to review daily, reinforcing your objectives to your conscious and
subconscious mind. But goals alone are not enough. It's also vital that you take time to
identify your Most Important Next Step (M.I.N.S.) for each goal, so your goal transforms
into an action. And remember, when it comes to M.I.N.S., be specific.

Real Estate Goal: _____

Weekly Objective: _____

M.I.N.S. _____

Second Goal: _____

Weekly Objective: _____

M.I.N.S. _____

Third Goal: _____

Weekly Objective: _____

M.I.N.S. _____

I can consider today a "win" if I _____

Now, go place this on your time-blocking calendar for today.

REAL ESTATE L.A.P.S. FUNNEL

Use this space to set a daily goal for
defining how you'll get **leads**, how many
properties you'll **analyze**, how many
properties you'll **pursue** (offer), and how
many you'll **purchase** today.

GOAL   REALITY

LEADS

ANALYZE

PURSUE

$

TODAY'S TIME-BLOCKING ACTIVITIES

High-achieving real estate investors know that what gets scheduled gets done.
Take a few minutes to think about your goals, your M.I.N.S., and schedule your day.
Don't forget to include several breaks.

5AM–6AM _____   2PM–3PM _____

6AM–7AM _____   3PM–4PM _____

7AM–8AM _____   4PM–5PM _____

8AM–9AM _____   5PM–6PM _____

9AM–10AM _____   6PM–7PM _____

10AM–11AM _____   7PM–8PM _____

11AM–12PM _____   8PM–9PM _____

12PM–1PM _____   9PM–10PM _____

1PM–2PM _____   10PM–11PM _____

☐ Did I include enough breaks
   in the day?

☐ Did I schedule my #1 most
   important thing?

EVENING REVIEW

Today was awesome because _____

_____

Today I struggled with _____

_____

On a scale of 1–10, with 10 being the highest, I would rate today's
productivity at a...   1   2   3   4   5   6   7   8   9   10

Tomorrow I will...   Other Thoughts/Notes

_____   _____

_____   _____

_____   _____

_____   _____

_____   _____

_____   _____

NOTES

NOTES

NOTES

NOTES

NOTES

NOTES

NOTES

NOTES

CONGRATULATIONS!

You made it to the end of your
90 Days of Intention Journal!

At this point, I hope you've learned the secret that all high-achievers know: It's not just about the goal, it's about the person you become in pursuit of that goal. It is my hope that after 90 days of intention, you have transformed into a better version of yourself—someone with a future that looks brighter than it did 90 days ago.

Of course, your journey doesn't end here. Success doesn't depend on chance or luck, but on years of consistent intention. While one 90-day journey is complete, another is just beginning—it's time to reset some big goals and conquer them over the next several months!

Thank you for including BiggerPockets in your journey. We hope you'll continue to stick close to us as you transform into the person you are about to become.

Your friend at BiggerPockets,

Brandon Turner

P.S. If you haven't picked up your newest journal, I invite you to do so now by visiting BiggerPockets.com/journal. Use code REORDER to save 15% on the next one!